New Mermaids

General editor: Brian Gibb[...]
Professor of English Literature, Unive[...] Münster

The Alchemist

All for Love

Arden of Faversham

Bartholmew Fair

The Beaux' Stratagem

The Changeling

A Chaste Maid in Cheapside

The Country Wife

The Critic

Dr Faustus

The Duchess of Malfi

The Dutch Courtesan

Eastward Ho!

Edward the Second

Epicoene or The Silent Woman

Every Man In His Humour

Gammer Gurton's Needle

An Ideal Husband

The Importance of Being Earnest

The Jew of Malta

The Knight of the Burning Pestle

Lady Windermere's Fan

Love for Love

The Malcontent

The Man of Mode

Marriage A-la-Mode

A New Way to Pay Old Debts

The Old Wife's Tale

The Playboy of the Western World

The Provoked Wife

The Recruiting Officer

The Relapse

The Revenger's Tragedy

The Rivals

The Roaring Girl

The Rover

The School for Scandal

She Stoops to Conquer

The Shoemaker's Holiday

The Spanish Tragedy

Tamburlaine

Three Late Medieval Morality Plays

  Mankind

  Everyman

  Mundus et Infans

'Tis Pity She's a Whore

Volpone

The Way of the World

The White Devil

The Witch

The Witch of Edmonton

A Woman Killed with Kindness

A Woman of No Importance

Women Beware Women

JOHN FORD

'Tis Pity She's a Whore

Edited by Martin Wiggins

*Fellow and Senior Lecturer, The Shakespeare Institute,
University of Birmingham*

A & C BLACK • LONDON
W W NORTON • NEW YORK

Second edition 2003

Reprinted 2004, 2005 (twice)
A & C Black Publishers Limited
37 Soho Square, London W1D 3QZ
www.acblack.com

ISBN-10: 0–7136–5060–5
ISBN-13: 978-0-7136-5060-0

First New Mermaid edition 1968 by Ernest Benn Limited

Published in the United States of America by
W. W. Norton & Company Inc.
500 Fifth Avenue, New York, N.Y. 10110

ISBN 0-393-90067-7

CIP catalogue records for this book are available
from the British Library and the Library of Congress

Printed in Great Britain by
Bookmarque Ltd, Croydon, Surrey

CONTENTS

ACKNOWLEDGEMENTS

I am grateful to Brian Gibbons for being such a patient and supportive General Editor, and to Katie Taylor for her corresponding patience and support at A & C Black. The following people helped with various aspects of the research, and the edition is the better for it: Roberta Barker, Tony Boyd-Williams, Anna Collins, Stephanie Gamble, Peter Holland, Sergio Mazzarelli, Anna Parker, Chris Penny, Jim Shaw, Sally Spurring, Brian Vickers, and Kate Welch. My colleagues Russell Jackson, John Jowett, and Catherine Richardson have been most generous with their learning and time. The Renaissance Drama Research Group of The Shakespeare Institute kept me company and kept me honest, and Kelley Costigan's contribution was, as always, immeasurable. None of them is responsible for any of my errors and infelicities.

What is mine, and worthwhile, in this edition is dedicated to the memory of Bosola, who died, aged 384 days, on the press night of the 1991 Royal Shakespeare Company production of *'Tis Pity She's a Whore.*

INTRODUCTION

THE AUTHOR

John Ford was born into a well-to-do and well-connected Devonshire family in the spring of 1586, and on Tuesday 12 April he was baptised at St Michael's church in his home town of Ilsington on the eastern edge of Dartmoor. He was the second son of six children: Henry, the eldest brother, who was about two years older than John; Thomas (baptised 6 September 1587); Elizabeth (baptised 11 January 1593); Edward (baptised 29 September 1596); and Jane, who is known only from a record of her burial. Their father, Thomas Ford, owned land in several local parishes, and their mother Elizabeth (née Popham) was a niece of the Attorney General John Popham (1531?–1607), who was later knighted and became the Lord Chief Justice. The Fords too were legally minded: in particular, Thomas senior's cousin, also Thomas Ford (1567–1635), eventually became a judge and a senior member of the Middle Temple, one of London's four eminent law societies known as the Inns of Court. Both Henry, in October 1600, and John, in November 1602, were also admitted to the Middle Temple as junior members. John remained there for most of his life: he was still a member in 1638, when the published edition of his comedy, *The Fancies, Chaste and Noble*, included commendatory verses addressed to 'Master John Ford of the Middle Temple'.

So Ford left home at the age of sixteen to live and study in London.[1] He joined an institution that was not only a prestigious law school but also a centre of literary and dramatic activity: a prominent junior member at the time of his arrival was the fashionable commercial playwright John Marston.[2] Initially, however, Ford had no discernible literary inclinations: it was not until 1606, at the age of twenty, that he wrote his first works for publication. It is tempting to link this with his money difficulties that year: in the spring he was expelled from the Middle Temple, apparently for failing to pay his buttery bill, and *Fame's Memorial* and *Honour Triumphant* appeared soon afterwards. Both works, celebrating noble lives and values, look like thinly disguised bids for patronage; the fact that the particular aristocrat honoured in *Fame's Memorial* was the late Earl of Devonshire suggests he may have been hoping that local connections would work in his favour. In

---

[1] A sixteen-year-old John Ford of Devon was admitted to Exeter College, Oxford on 26 March 1601, but this cannot be the dramatist, who had not yet reached his fifteenth birthday.

[2] For a fuller account of the atmosphere and environment of the Middle Temple at this time, see Philip J. Finkelpearl, *John Marston of the Middle Temple: An Elizabethan Dramatist in his Social Setting* (Cambridge, Mass., 1969).

any event, by June 1608 his financial affairs had become stable enough for him to petition for readmission to the Middle Temple, which was granted on payment of his debts and a £2 fine.

What we know of his London life during the ensuing years depends mainly on indirect or negative evidence. Only one document in the Middle Temple's records bears on his career there, and on closer examination it proves bedevilled by an insoluble ambiguity. In May 1617, the society suffered an outbreak of indiscipline after its authorities had refused a group of junior members' request to liberalize its dress code, which required the wearing of lawyers' caps at meals and in church. The four young men concerned wanted to wear hats instead, and, when rebuffed, chose to flout the rules. When they were threatened with expulsion, the Middle Temple erupted in protest: some members defiantly wore their hats at communal meals, while others absented themselves altogether and dined in their chambers, or at eating-houses in the town. The authorities cracked down on 30 May, formally censuring forty-nine members. The tenth name on the list (which is not arranged in order of seniority) is John Ford. But by now there were two John Fords at the Middle Temple: the second, a young man from Somerset, had been admitted the previous November. It is impossible to say for certain which of them the authorities meant to rebuke. If it was the poet, then he would have been one of the oldest participants in a primarily youthful rebellion: of the forty-eight others named, eighteen were admitted in 1616 and 1617, and only five before 1610. The odds favour the Somerset Ford, but we cannot rule out the poet, who was evidently capable of association with much younger men: later on, several of the friends who wrote commendatory verses for his published plays were around twenty years his junior. The same material suggests a circle of acquaintance far wider than the closed society of the Middle Temple: by the 1620s he could claim friendship with successful London dramatists like Webster and Massinger, with the sons of important men, and with lawyers in other Inns of Court, notably Gray's Inn where his cousin (yet another John Ford) was a member. Perhaps Ford, if it was he, became unwittingly embroiled in the 'hats' controversy simply because he was in the habit of eating out for other reasons.

It is not known what he was doing for a living at this time. He may have worked in some legal capacity, though there is no record that he was ever called to the bar. During the 1610s there was a trickle of literary writing: *A Funeral Elegy* (1612) on the death of William Peter, wrongly assigned by the publisher to one 'W.S.'; a prose tract, *The Golden Mean* (1613); a religious poem, *Christ's Bloody Sweat* (1613); a lost biography, probably in verse, of his murdered Middle Temple colleague, Sir Thomas Overbury (1615);

and a moralistic pamphlet, *A Line of Life* (1620).[3] At some time he also came into possession of two modest holdings of land in Devon. The death of his father in the spring of 1610 made little impact on his financial position, whatever it now was: Ford senior bequeathed his second son only a £10 lump sum, whereas the two younger sons were left annual incomes of the same amount. This has sometimes been interpreted as a sign that John had somehow incurred his father's displeasure, though it is also possible that by now he was well enough established in London not to need more than a token legacy. In any event, he received a little more when his brother Henry died in 1616 after less than four years of married life: apparently concerned to consolidate the family's Devonshire property in the hands of his heirs, he willed John an annuity of £20 in exchange for his two holdings of land. But this was not enough to make him independently wealthy: £20 a year would not have covered his living expenses at the Middle Temple.

We don't know precisely when he began to write plays. The question is related to the equally uncertain issue of what plays, extant and lost, make up his total dramatic canon. At its solid core are the seven that were published in authorized editions between 1629 and 1639: *The Lover's Melancholy*, *The Broken Heart*, *'Tis Pity She's a Whore*, *Love's Sacrifice*, *Perkin Warbeck*, *The Fancies*, *Chaste and Noble*, and *The Lady's Trial*. Two other published plays, written collaboratively, name him as part-author, and scholars over the years have attempted, sometimes convincingly and sometimes not, to attribute four more to him in whole or part. A further seven titles of lost plays are associated with him in seventeenth-century documents of varying credibility. Discounting the triumphs of hope over plausibility, John Ford probably had a hand in fifteen plays still known to us.[4]

Many of those fifteen are hard to date exactly, but from the available evidence there emerges a blurry picture of Ford's overall dramatic career. He probably started in the early 1620s as a junior writing partner of Thomas Dekker, a playwright of long experience who had recently

---

[3] Except for the *Funeral Elegy*, the extant writings are collected in L. E. Stock et al., *The Non-dramatic Works of John Ford* (Binghamton, New York, 1991). The attribution of the *Funeral Elegy* is discussed in Brian Vickers, *'Counterfeiting' Shakespeare: Evidence, Authorship, and John Ford's Funerall Elegye* (Cambridge, 2002).

[4] There seems little good reason to perpetuate the flimsy arguments for Ford's authorship of *The Queen* (published anonymously in 1653), nor the claims of a Stationers' Register entry of 1660 which names him as the author of the lost plays *The London Merchant, The Royal Combat, and An Ill Beginning Has a Good End and a Bad Beginning May Have a Good End*. Doubts about the latter's testimony are amply justified by the fact that it also assigns the otherwise unknown *King Stephen, Duke Humphrey,* and *Iphis and Iantha* to William Shakespeare. The conjecture that Ford may have contributed scenes to Dekker's *The Welsh Ambassador* (1623) is more attractive, but still unsupported by any firm evidence.

emerged white-haired from seven years out of circulation in a London debtors' prison. Ford may have come to know him through John Webster, who had himself been Dekker's junior collaborator about fifteen years earlier (and whose father had, incidentally, been one of Dekker's creditors at the time of his arrest); Webster probably knew Ford as a fellow writer of Overbury memorial verse, which was almost a little industry in mid-1610s literary culture. In 1621, Ford and Dekker joined the comic actor William Rowley to produce *The Witch of Edmonton*, a tragedy based on a recent murder case. Their four other known collaborations all date from 1624: *The Sun's Darling*, a 'moral masque' and the only survivor of the four; *The Fairy Knight*; *The Late Murder in Whitechapel*, a speed-written tragedy to which Webster and Rowley also contributed; and *The Bristol Merchant*. Meanwhile Ford began an association with the King's Men, England's principal acting company: he wrote the tragicomedy *The Laws of Candy* for them at some time before 1623, possibly working from an outline provided by a more experienced playwright, and in late 1625 he joined Webster and Massinger as part of a syndicate of writers hired to finish off *The Fair Maid of the Inn*, the last work of the recently dead house dramatist, John Fletcher. A few years later, he began to write without a collaborator, and the King's Men staged his first three plays: the tragicomedy *The Lover's Melancholy* (1628), the tragedy *The Broken Heart* (1629?), and the lost *Beauty in a Trance* (1630?), which may have been a comedy. Thereafter he wrote exclusively for the companies managed by Christopher Beeston (d. 1638) at the Phoenix theatre in Drury Lane: *'Tis Pity* for Queen Henrietta's Men, along with *Love's Sacrifice* (1632?), *Perkin Warbeck* (1633?), and *The Fancies, Chaste and Noble* (1635?); and, for Beeston's Boys, *The Lady's Trial* (1638). After publishing the last of these in 1639, Ford disappears from history. It is not known when, where, or how he died.[5]

MAKING *'Tis Pity She's a Whore*: SOURCES, DATE, AND EARLY PRODUCTIONS

Except for his historical tragedy of *Perkin Warbeck*, Ford tended to devise his own plots, so *'Tis Pity She's a Whore* has no single, clear-cut

[5] In 1873 a copy of the 1635 edition of Angel Day's *The English Secretary* was reported as having the title-page inscription 'Johne Ford Middle Tempil 15 Jully 1641' (X. X., 'John Ford, the Dramatist', *Notes and Queries*, 4th series, 11 [1873], 403), but the spelling suggests the *faux*-antiquarianism of a later forgery rather than genuine seventeenth-century orthography. A tradition that Ford retired to Devonshire in his old age has no reliable pedigree earlier than the 1820s, when interest in the dramatist was starting to revive after more than a century of neglect.

narrative source: in the process of composition he synthesized situations, scenes, and character relationships from a range of material. He may well have found a hint for the initial scenario, with the suitors seeking Annabella's hand in marriage, in John Florio's Italian phrase-book, *First Fruits* (1578). The section devoted to 'Amorous talk' includes a conversation where a would-be lover describes the object of his passion: like Annabella, 'She is a maid, daughter unto a merchant of this city, so famous and great.'[6] Florio also gave Ford a name for the merchant, as well as a few phrases quoted in the play (one of them on the very next page of 'Amorous talk'). Two of the suitors also took their names from an old book: George Whetstone's *Heptameron of Civil Discourses* (1582) includes characters called Soranso and Bargetto. The incest plot inlaid in this situation has some parallels with a story in Francois de Rosset's *Histoires Tragiques de Notre Temps* (Paris, 1615), about the sexual relationship between a brilliant student and his older, married sister; Rosset also supplied the name Richardetto.

In filling in the outlines of his story, Ford drew on what was to him classic modern drama. Simple theatrical necessity may dictate that a forbidden love needs confidants to give the lovers someone else to discuss it with and the play another angle of approach, but Ford's decision to make these figures a friar and a female servant, both of an older generation, must have been made with Shakespeare's *Romeo and Juliet* (1595–6) in mind.[7] As we shall see, parallels with and deviations from the Elizabethan tragedy sometimes influence the way we respond to the situation in Ford's play, and these would certainly have been recognizable to the original audience: Caroline theatrical culture had a strong nostalgic element, so the plays of the previous generation were frequently revived, and new dramatic writing often felt the weight of an established canon bearing down upon it.[8] Ford himself is often characterized as a 'belated' writer who only arrived in London as a teenager after the first production of *Hamlet* (1600) and who only began to write plays in his mid-thirties after the golden Shakespearian quarter-century of English Renaissance drama had come to an end. Scholars have accordingly been prone to see echoes of that earlier drama in *'Tis Pity She's a Whore*. Sometimes these are unmistakable. In the 1630s any climactic scene of tragic love and murder could scarcely avoid comparison with *Othello* (1604), then Shakespeare's most popular and influential play, and Giovanni's

---

[6] *First Fruits*, D1r.

[7] For a thorough study of Ford's debt to Shakespeare's play, see R. L. Smallwood, '*'Tis Pity She's a Whore* and *Romeo* and *Juliet*', *Cahiers Elisabéthains* 20 (1981), 49–70.

[8] Martin Wiggins, 'The King's Men and After', in Jonathan Bate and Russell Jackson (eds.), *Shakespeare: An Illustrated Stage History* (Oxford, 1996), pp. 38–9.

killing Annabella 'in a kiss' (V.v.84) is a direct parallel (compare *Othello* V.ii.368–9).[9] Similarly, in Annabella's incarceration and her communication with the outside world using a letter written in her own blood and dropped from her balcony, Ford imitated what was probably the oldest play still in the Caroline repertory, Thomas Kyd's blood-and-thunder classic *The Spanish Tragedy* (c. 1586), in which Bel-Imperia receives similar treatment. But other suggested links are more tendentious, though sometimes suggestive; in particular, there are local parallels with two plays by Ford's fellow Middle Templar John Marston. The scenic device of Annabella and confidante watching her suitors from the stage balcony (I.ii) was previously used in Marston's *Antonio and Mellida* (1600), and Ford may also have been struck by Antonio's, admittedly conventional, love rhetoric in the same scene:

> Could your quick eye strike through these gashèd wounds,
> You should behold a heart, a heart, fair creature,
> Raging more wild than is this frantic sea. (I.i.227–9)

It is an image that recurs throughout Ford's play, gradually shedding its metaphorical trappings until it becomes gruesomely literal at the climax: in their first scene together, Giovanni tells his sister,

> Rip up my bosom: there thou shalt behold
> A heart in which is writ the truth I speak, (I.ii.205–6)

and Lord Soranzo too avers, 'Did you but see my heart . . .' (III.ii.24). Annabella's eventual concession to Soranzo, 'If I hereafter find that I must marry, / It shall be you or none' (III.ii.62–3) in turn echoes Marston's *The Dutch Courtesan* (1605), in which Crispinella tells a suitor, with similar evasiveness, 'if ever I marry it shall be you, and I will marry, and yet I hope I do not say it shall be you neither' (IV.i.66–7), while her sister Beatrice shares a concern expressed by Giovanni: 'Sister, shall we know one another in the other world?' (IV.iv.65–6; compare *'Tis Pity* V.v.36–7).[10]

---

[9] The links between the two plays are explored in detail in Raymond Powell, 'The Adaptation of a Shakespearean Genre: *Othello* and Ford's *'Tis Pity She's a Whore*', *Renaissance Quarterly* 48 (1995), 582–92.

[10] For further suggestions about Ford's use of earlier drama, see Richard S. Ide, 'Ford's *'Tis Pity She's a Whore* and the Benefits of Belatedness' and Mark Stavig, 'Shakespearean and Jacobean Patterns in *'Tis Pity She's a Whore*', both in Donald K. Anderson, jun. (ed.), *'Concord in Discord': The Plays of John Ford, 1586–1986* (New York, 1986), pp. 61–86, 221–40.

What is striking about these various source materials is their early date. Most of them were written in or soon after the reign of Queen Elizabeth, and many were long out of print at the time Ford was working as a dramatist.[11] (Florio's *First Fruits* was only ever printed once, in 1578.) In his research for this tragedy it seems that he deliberately looked at rather old books, and the text itself contains many details, which would have been more obvious in the 1630s than they are now, indicating that he intended it as a period piece set in the recent past. Putana's remark that Grimaldi has served in a war between the Papal states and Milan (I.ii.77) casually places the play in mid-sixteenth-century Italian history, and Soranzo's taste for the love poems of Sannazaro (II.ii) suggests the same, but unspoken details say the most. Nobody in Ford's day wore a codpiece, as Bergetto does, and no seventeenth-century aristocratic wedding had a masque so simple as the one given in honour of Soranzo and Annabella in IV.i. Most telling of all is the fact that no character ever uses or even mentions a gun: firearms were commonplace weapons in Caroline plays set in contemporary times, but this one rigorously sticks to rapier and dagger.

Ford's reason for choosing a period setting probably lay in his under-standing of Renaissance literary theory. One of the ways this differentiated between the two principal dramatic genres was in terms of the historicity or otherwise of the stories they told: comic plots were fictitious, whereas tragic events had actually happened, and so were the more piteous and terrible. Thus in the prologues to his comedies, Ford tends to insist on the originality of his own invention, whereas the usually no less invented scenarios of his tragedies are said to have a basis in reality: as he puts it in *The Broken Heart*,

> What may be here thought a fiction, when time's youth
> Wanted some riper years was known a truth.[12]

Tragedy is conceived as the present-day residue of real human lives, as the sufferings of one age turn into sad stories for another: in *'Tis Pity She's a Whore*, the imprisoned Annabella, recognizing that she is doomed, antici-pates the way that, in 'ages that are yet unborn', her life will become 'A wretched, woeful woman's tragedy' (V.i.7–8) – in fact, the very tragedy which the theatre audience is watching.

---

[11] The Friar's description of hell (III.vi.8–23), moreover, is ultimately drawn from a passage in Thomas Nashe's prose pamphlet *Pierce Penniless* (1592), though Ford's immediate source may have been his own previous imitation in *Christ's Bloody Sweat*.

[12] Ford, *The Broken Heart*, prol. 15–16.

Naturally all this is a hindrance to scholars in determining exactly when the play was written: the source material is remote from Ford's own time and there are no contemporary allusions. The overall pattern of his work during the late 1620s and early 1630s gives scope for a hypothesis – he seems to have written one play a year between 1628 and 1633, with 1631 suggestively vacant – but the only piece of external evidence is maddeningly opaque: in the dedication to the printed edition of 1633, he speaks of *'Tis Pity* as 'these first fruits of my leisure'. Some scholars infer that it was his first play written without a collaborator, before his three Blackfriars plays of 1628–30, but others think it was simply the first product of some indeterminable period of 'leisure'. It is possible that this leisure followed the end of his (perhaps contractual) relationship with the King's Men, when he was free to write for whichever company he chose. He may not even have had a particular company in mind: the play demands no unusual stage facilities, and though a lot of props are required, they are mostly commonplace objects that would have been part of any well-equipped company's stock; only Annabella's heart would need to be specially procured.

In any event, the play was staged for the sophisticated, socially elevated audiences who frequented Christopher Beeston's Phoenix theatre. The resident company, Queen Henrietta's Men, numbered fourteen principal actors, plus boy apprentices, which would have been ample for Ford's modest casting requirements. Its leading man was Richard Perkins (d. 1650), who had been acting since 1602; what we know of his career indicates a performer of some range, from scheming villains to concerned fathers, and his likeliest roles would have been Vasques or Florio. (Vasques is the better of the two parts, but by the 1630s acting companies tended not to concentrate all their most rewarding roles in the hands of a single star actor.) The female parts would all have been taken by male actors: the young women, Annabella, Hippolita, and Philotis, would certainly have been played by boys, and perhaps also Putana, though it was not unknown for an adult male actor to play an older woman.[13]

The playhouse itself had an indoor stage and auditorium lit by candles, which were trimmed during the act-intervals while music was played; early performances were thus divided into five sections rather than the two of modern convention. The candles may also have enabled the company to control the level of stage light in a way that was not possible in outdoor theatres, so that nocturnal sequences like the end of Act III could be played

[13] It is especially telling that a character similar to Putana, Nurse Keep in Ben Jonson's *The Magnetic Lady* (1632), was probably played by a man: an experienced playwright like Jonson would not have directed the Nurse to carry her fourteen-year-old charge Placentia across the stage had he expected the role to be played by a boy.

in relative (though probably not absolute) darkness. The stage had three main entrances set across the back façade, two of them doors and the middle one a large curtained alcove known as the discovery space, which enabled large props (such as Annabella's bed in V.v) to be brought onto the stage and could also be set with scenery to represent a confined space like Soranzo's and the Friar's studies in II.ii and Ill.vi respectively. There was also a stage balcony, used in three scenes (I.ii, III.ii, and V.i) and large enough to accommodate at least two actors.

We have no eye-witness accounts of the play in production at the Phoenix, although it seems to have been successful: the 1633 edition mentions 'the general commendation deserved by the actors in their presentment of this tragedy'. There is a good chance that it was performed on one of the forty-nine occasions that Queen Henrietta's Men appeared at court between 1629 and 1633, which may have been where it was seen by the 1633 edition's dedicatee, the Earl of Peterborough; it may also have been part of the company's touring repertory during the early 1630s. However, it evidently belonged to the theatre's manager, Beeston, rather than to the acting company, and it passed to his own troupe, Beeston's Boys, after they became the resident Phoenix company in 1637. The play was still associated with the Beeston family in 1661, when it was performed at the Salisbury Court theatre owned by Christopher's son William. Samuel Pepys saw it there on Monday 9 September, and thought it 'a simple [foolish] play, and ill acted'; he was more interested in the 'most pretty and most ingenious lady' sitting next to him in the audience.[14] She would have had some female competition on stage: the actors, led by George Jolly, were the first English professional troupe to employ women, so this production would have featured the first Annabella played by an actress; sadly her identity is unknown.[15] The company later set up as a touring operation with 'Tis Pity as part of its repertory of pre-Civil War plays; there is a record of a performance at the King's Arms, Norwich in 1663. It was not seen again on any English stage until 1923.

INCEST, INTELLECTUALISM, AND IDEOLOGY

William Gifford expressed the consensus of several centuries when he wrote in 1811 that 'Tis Pity She's a Whore 'carries with it insuperable obstacles to

[14] Samuel Pepys, *The Diary*, ed. Robert Latham and William Matthews (London, 1970–83), ii. 175.
[15] Elizabeth Howe, *The First English Actresses: Women and Drama, 1660–1700* (Cambridge, 1992), p. 23.

its appearance upon a modern stage'.[16] To an extent, those obstacles arise out of Anglo-Saxon reticence about sexual matters in general: it is no surprise that the more sophisticated French should have taken the lead in the play's return to the repertory, with Maurice Maeterlinck's adaptation, *Annabella*, staged in Paris in 1894.[17] In the twentieth century, it benefited from the upheavals in European society during the 1960s, including the abolition of theatre censorship in Britain and the growing acceptability of sexual frankness in the arts: in 1973, Giuseppe Patroni Griffi directed a heavily adapted film version whose cinematography paid attention to the beauty of the nude human body as well as of landscape and architecture (when it was released on video in 1993, it was marketed as a European sex-and-horror flick), and on stage the high water mark of sexual candour was a 1977 studio production directed by Ron Daniels for the Royal Shakespeare Company, in which Giovanni and Annabella made love naked on stage.[18] By the end of the 1970s, the play was firmly established, perhaps for the first time, as a classic of the stage as well as the study, one of the few non-Shakespearian works of its time to have been produced by both the leading British companies, the RSC and the National Theatre.[19] Yet as the limits of tolerance and taste narrowed in the last two decades of the century, productions tended to become more cautious and restrained in their treatment of the incest elements: the play returned to the National Theatre and the RSC, in 1988 and 1991 respectively, in versions giving little overt attention to the lovers' sexuality, and though they had their first sexual encounter on stage in the last major production of the twentieth century, directed by David Lan at the Young Vic in 1999, they were masked from the audience by the black cloaks of other actors.

The play's title in particular continues to create difficulty: there are tales of student productions being unable to advertise in newsagents' windows, and as recently as 1988 the National Theatre found it impossible to obtain commercial sponsorship for Alan Ayckbourn's production without renaming the play. They didn't, but the incident shows how little has changed in some quarters since 1831, when the text was omitted from a collection of Ford's *Dramatic Works* which appeared in John Murray's 'Family Library'

---

[16] William Gifford, *Quarterly Review* 6 (1811), 466.

[17] The play proper also received a string of Paris productions in 1934, 1948, and 1961, well in advance of its popularity on British stages; the last, directed by Luchino Visconti, featured lavish stage design and an exceptionally glamorous pair of lovers in Romy Schneider and Alain Delon.

[18] Further details of major modern productions in Britain in the twentieth century are given on pp. 38–40.

[19] The National Theatre first produced the play in 1972.

series: in his introductory discussion of Ford's career, the anonymous editor also chose to call the play *Annabella and Giovanni*, explaining in a footnote that 'This title has been substituted for a much coarser one.'[20] This sort of behaviour can only partly be put down to moronic prudery. The play has been making some readers squirm for centuries: one critic in 1891 went so far as to say that it could not be appreciated 'by any well-regulated mind' – in Victorian terms, virtually an imputation of obscenity.[21] The problem was acutely articulated two hundred years earlier by the first great scholar of English drama, Gerard Langbaine: he noted that the play 'were to be commended, did not the author paint the incestuous love between Giovanni and his sister Annabella in too beautiful colours'.[22] The play often provokes a conflict in sensibilities which results in embarrassed discomfort and strong emotions: 'though the language . . . is eminently beautiful,' wrote the clergyman editor Alexander Dyce in 1869, 'the plot is repulsive'.[23] In other words, these critics felt that the play's literary qualities seemed to prescribe a response that was offensive to their preconceived moral codes.

Ford often writes the incestuous relationship in the conventional terminology of romantic love, such as when Giovanni first broaches it to his sister:

> I have too long suppressed the hidden flames
> That almost have consumed me. I have spent
> Many a silent night in sighs and groans,
> Ran over all my thoughts, despised my fate,
> Reasoned against the reasons of my love,
> Done all that smoothed-cheek Virtue could advise,
> But found all bootless: 'tis my destiny
> That you must either love, or I must die. (I.ii.217–24)

What can make this disturbing for some readers and playgoers is the representation of a brother proposing incest in the same register as any young lover torturing himself with the fear of rejection: the flames of passion, sleepless nights, and contemplated suicide are all familiar from the Renaissance love poetry of Petrarch and his imitators. But then, what else would you expect? One of Giovanni's more compelling points is that his

---

[20] John Ford, *The Dramatic Works* (London, 1831), vol. i, p. xviii n.

[21] Frederick Gard Fleay, *A Biographical Chronicle of the English Drama, 1559–1642* (London, 1891), i. 233.

[22] Gerard Langbaine, *An Account of the English Dramatick Poets* (Oxford, 1691), p. 222.

[23] John Ford, *The Works*, ed. Alexander Dyce (London, 1869), i. 108 n.

emotional experience is the same as that of any other lover: 'Must I not do what all men else may – love?' (I.i.19) Accordingly, the language is doing the same job of expressing those feelings as it would with any other lover; it is only the particular circumstances of this couple which makes an ethical difference.

The issue is not allowed to remain latent, and so potentially ignorable. One of the distinctive qualities of 'Tis Pity She's a Whore is that its drama is not only experiential but also intellectual: it overtly represents a conflict of ideas as well as of human beings. Giovanni and the Friar are academically gifted characters, student and tutor of the University of Bologna, to whom reason and argument are second nature. Instead of the essays, tutorials, and seminars of university life today, students of this period were trained through formal disputations, known as 'exercises', in which they would apply their skills in grammar, logic, and rhetoric to prove or disprove a given proposition. The proposition itself didn't matter except as a focus for debate: logical 'proof' did not necessarily establish empirical truth, because that was not the point of the exercise; the objective was simply to develop the students' faculties for arguing a case one way or the other. It is a system which has clearly shaped Giovanni: he is always offering to 'prove' things by systematic rational analysis, usually as a way of justifying some act or idea.

This is where the play begins, with Giovanni treating incest as if it were a disputation topic, a problem in abstract logic. Homing in astutely on the external prohibitions of religious law, he seeks first to argue them away as nothing more than a pointlessly restrictive social taboo: the terms *brother* and *sister* are 'a peevish sound, / A customary form, from man to man' (I.i.24–5) with no substantive meaning in themselves; the implication is that the concept of sibling incest is equally arbitrary. A corollary is that he speaks of his living father in the past tense: 'Say that we had one father, say one womb / . . . gave both us life and birth' (I.i.28–9). The one undeniable nexus between brother and sister is a point of origin, but to make incest permissible, that has to be kept firmly in the past: *father* can mean no more than the man who once sired them, so that their relationship is one of simple biological affinity rather than continuing kinship. The second stage of the argument takes that biological affinity as the basis of a positive case *for* incest: since they share their parentage,

> Are we not therefore each to other bound
> So much the more by nature, by the links
> Of blood, of reason (nay, if you will have't,
> Even of religion), to be ever one,
> One soul, one flesh, one love, one heart, one all? (I.i.30–4)

Annabella (Saskia Reeves) and Giovanni (Jonathan Cullen) after consummating their relationship, Act II, scene i, in the 1991 Royal Shakespeare Company production directed by David Leveaux; Joe Cocks Studio Collection © Shakespeare Birthplace Trust

In other words, because siblings are naturally like one another, it is also natural, and reasonable, that they should love one another as much as they love themselves: 'one flesh' leads to 'one love'. Vocabulary here bridges what might otherwise seem a surprising leap in the argument from genetic similarity to incest, since 'one flesh' was also a well-known biblical way of expressing the relationship between husband and wife: if brothers and sisters too are one flesh, then they must have the same privileges and duties as a married couple, including what was then considered the duty of sexual consummation.

This is slippery logic, dependent on unspoken ambiguities and trying to have it all ways. In the theatre, where we don't have the chance to stop and scrutinize the argument in detail, the crucial question is what balance the actor strikes between conveying its inherent weaknesses on the one hand and, on the other, the degree of personal conviction with which Giovanni presents his case: he can be portrayed as a genius, foolish rather than wise in his worldliness, driven by a misplaced confidence in the real-life application of academic ratiocination; or as a clever but intellectually dishonest obsessive trying to rationalize a predetermined course of action. The choice is important because it affects how we interpret the one moment when Giovanni obviously misleads his sister:

> I have asked counsel of the holy Church,
> Who tells me I may love you. (I.ii.236–7)

That is, of course, not true – the Friar said only 'you may love' (I.i.20), without a qualifying pronoun – but it depends on the characterization of Giovanni whether it is a deliberate lie or a tendentious refashioning of the truth by someone who honestly believes in the power of human reason to change reality. In this connection it is important that in all other respects the liaison is shown to be completely consensual at its inception: 'what thou hast urged,' says Annabella, 'My captive heart had long ago resolved.' (I.ii.240–1) Were it not for their prior social and biological relationship, the starting-point of Giovanni's positive case, this would be an utterly normal, appealing case of romantic love: the play's similarities to *Romeo and Juliet*, obvious to sophisticated audiences from the 1630s to the present day, are very much to the point. Giovanni ultimately proposes that the human authenticity of the experience should override the moral precepts which classify it:

> If ever after-times should hear
> Of our fast-knit affections, though perhaps
> The laws of conscience and of civil use

> May justly blame us, yet when they but know
> Our loves, that love will wipe away that rigour
> Which would in other incests be abhorred.   (V.v.68–73)

The mismatch between the two ways of responding raises awkward questions; some of the play's earlier readers would evidently have been more comfortable if these had remained unasked.

Part of the problem is that the play, and indeed human moral culture in general, cannot offer Giovanni an intellectually adequate answer. Prohibitions of sibling incest always end up having to invoke the arbitrary dictates of some higher authority such as nature or God. The only rebuttal the Friar can make is to give up arguing: 'Dispute no more in this,' he tells his pupil, 'These are no school points' (I.i.1–2). Like St Bonaventura, the thirteenth-century scholastic philosopher after whom he is named, his fundamental position is that truths revealed by God, even to the mind of a fool, are superior to the truths which may be discovered by the most brilliant processes of empirical human reasoning: thus he dismisses Giovanni's arguments as 'ignorance in knowledge' (II.v.27). Throughout the play, his only counter-position is to call attention to the divine sanction of hell with which he vividly terrifies Annabella into repentance (III.vi.8–30), but this has no basis in authenticated empirical experience, only in cultural tradition: seventeenth-century audiences knew from *Hamlet* that the afterlife, if there is one, is an 'undiscovered country from whose bourn / No traveller returns'.[24]

Many of the characters casually assume the existence of a dimension beyond the material – Vasques and Annabella both speak of their attendant 'good genii' (II.ii.154, V.i.31), and Richardetto supposes that 'there is one / Above begins to work' (IV.ii.8–9) in the failure of Soranzo's marriage – but if there really are such metaphysical beings mingling with the action, they are 'not with mortal eyes / To be beheld' (IV.i.4–5), as the Friar has to admit when he claims that the saints are guests at the wedding feast. In the play's performance history, attempts to realize such elements on the stage have tended to detract from its intellectual content, because they too easily belie Giovanni's philosophical development away from the others' non-rational belief in the supernatural: the sinister black-hooded figures who patrolled the margins of the 1999 Young Vic production implied, as one reviewer noted, 'a belief in hellfire that Ford's play resolutely declines to state'.[25] Initially Giovanni may take the Friar's admonitions seriously and offer up

---

[24] William Shakespeare, *Hamlet*, III.i.81–2.
[25] Jeremy Kingston, *The Times*, 9 October 1999.

fruitless prayers to avert divine vengeance, but by the end he is rejecting scholastic assertions about the end of the world and the hell to follow as mere 'slavish and fond superstitious fear' (V.iii.20): custom and tradition are now just 'Busy opinion' (1), to be accepted only if he can himself see their empirical justification. This is the point at which the Friar ultimately has to concede defeat: appeal to authority has been his sole argument, and once Giovanni no longer finds that intellectually valid, the only recourse is to leave Parma and abandon him to his fate.

To sum up, *'Tis Pity She's a Whore* enacts a debate between orthodox Christian revelation and the new sceptical empiricism of Renaissance philosophy, with Giovanni's incest placed at the sharp end: it is a relationship forbidden by every canon of received morality, but not one to which there is any obvious rational objection in terms of actual, material harm. The two underlying systems of thought are intellectually irreconcilable, and many of the play's perceived problems arise out of a desire that dramatically it should nonetheless reach a definite resolution favouring one side or the other – in effect, that it should take up a position about the difficult issues it raises by directing audience sympathy unambiguously. The play's earlier Christian readers obviously wanted it to support their preferred ideology and condemn incest, and they were (to say the least) disappointed. More recently, critics and directors have wanted to present the lovers as innocents manipulated and condemned by a grotesquely corrupt society, and to romanticize Giovanni in heroic terms, 'battling with Christianity', as Jude Law put it when he played the part at the Young Vic in 1999.[26] As we shall see, that doesn't work either.

THE LOVERS AND THE WORLD

The rather narrow focus of this discussion so far illustrates one of the oddities of *'Tis Pity's* construction as a work of art: the way some of its major intellectual concerns seem barely to impinge on the thread of its narrative. If Giovanni and the Friar are the central players in the confrontation between the old philosophy and the new, they are also placed on the sidelines of the story rather than at its centre: throughout the action, neither of them speaks at length to anyone but each other and Annabella, while the plot mainly goes on elsewhere. Giovanni has nevertheless been the role of choice for many a star actor, from Donald Wolfit in 1940 onwards: it has attracted, as well as Jude Law, Edward de Souza in 1961, Ian McKellen in

---

[26] Jude Law, quoted by Oliver Bennett, 'Law of Averages', *The Independent Magazine*, 25 September 1999, 7.

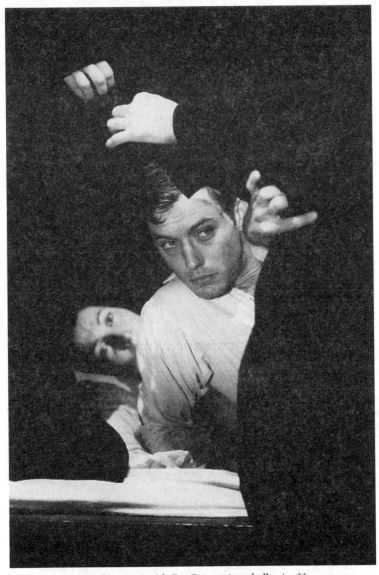

Jude Law as Giovanni with Eve Best as Annabella, Act V, scene v,
in the 1999 Young Vic production directed by David Lan;
Colin Willoughby/ArenaPAL

1972, Rupert Graves at the National Theatre in 1988, and Val Kilmer in New York in 1992, all of them prominent names in twentieth-century theatre and film. Yet for all the lines and stage time it offers, it is a role which consistently seems to disappoint. Wolfit dropped the play from his company's repertory after its few London performances, and subsequent actors have generally not found the heroic stature which is often expected of the part: in production, the role has more often conveyed petulance than power. Generations of theatre reviewers, looking for intellectual and emotional grandeur, have carped at the boyish immaturity of successive Giovannis: it was said that Nicholas Clay, who played the role in the National Theatre's first production in 1972, 'in adversity . . . merely seems to have a fit of the sulks'; Simon Rouse, who affected teenage acne in the 1977 RSC production, was dismissed as 'a pale schoolboy'; Tristram Wymark, at the Glasgow Citizens' Theatre in 1988, was 'a petulant, arrogant, sub-Byronic boy'; and in 1999 Jude Law was 'like an undergraduate going through an unstable phase', who 'does little except roll about on the floor and snivel a lot'.[27] The point is made most clearly in a review of Ian McKellen's performance in the 1972 Actors' Company production: 'he moves from frustrated unhappiness to a childish defiance of the Church, moping rather than being carried terribly onwards by passion. He eats cornets, wears lovely clothes, and mopes like a dissatisfied child. It is hardly Giovanni.'[28] But when good actors have repeatedly found those very qualities in the part, perhaps it *is* Giovanni after all: perhaps the failure is one of preconception rather than performances, and the character just isn't designed to be the conventional tragic hero he is often taken for.

It is worth remembering that, in its one moment approaching self-consciousness, the play lays its emphasis elsewhere: it is 'A wretched, woeful woman's tragedy.' (V.i.8) Giovanni may be the longer role, but Annabella has the more structurally central position in the narrative: the early stages juxtapose the progress of the incestuous relationship with the competitive wooing of her three other suitors, and the subsidiary murder intrigues involving Hippolita and Grimaldi radiate out from that. The facts of human biology and the patriarchal organization of Renaissance society mean that it is Annabella who suffers the immediate physical consequences of extramarital sex – pregnancy and brutal treatment by a jealous husband – and the play's title places her carnal degradation as the cause of tragic pity.

---

[27] John Barber, *Daily Telegraph,* 19 July 1972; Terry Grimley, *Birmingham Post,* 22 July 1977; Robert Dawson Scott, *The Times,* 23 February 1988; John Peter, *Sunday Times,* 17 October 1999, Charles Spencer, *Daily Telegraph,* 11 October 1999.
[28] Nicholas de Jongh, *The Guardian,* 6 September 1972.

In performance, tellingly, Annabellas tend to prove more successful than Giovannis. From the 'dew and flame' of Rosalind Iden, Wolfit's Annabella, twentieth-century actresses mined the role's contradictory complexities: directed by David Thompson at the Mermaid Theatre in 1961, Zena Walker conveyed 'both the intensity of her passion and the depth of her horror at it'; in the RSC's second production of the play, in 1991, Saskia Reeves, portrayed 'a woman rent apart between conventional fears and continued love of her brother'; and Eve Best, playing opposite Jude Law at the Young Vic in 1999, was 'a mild, wilting figure of non-specific pathos, who cannot deal with the strong emotions that she arouses in herself', and whose 'hands hover above her brother's body like a strimmer on a lawn', wanting, but not quite daring, to touch.[29] These performances astutely located Annabella as the play's hinge, half in her brother's world of sexual self-indulgence but also, crucially, half out of it, placed in a wider social world and subject to the moderating demands of its conventional sexual morality.

A corollary of Annabella's centrality is that directors wanting to focus the play on incest have to make some fairly drastic adaptations, usually streamlining the busy action surrounding the prenuptial negotiations. An extreme example is Griffi's film version, which removes virtually the entire wooing (only the successful suitor Soranzo appears), whilst also building up the incest strand by making Giovanni (Oliver Tobias) spend a week at the bottom of a well trying to kill off his illicit desires. In the text itself, the lovers slip more easily towards an early consummation between the first two acts, when the play has barely finished its initial exposition; Romeo and Juliet, in contrast, are halfway through their play before they consummate their love. Ford's lovers do not require the same kind of extended build-up because, as brother and sister in the same household, they already have physical access, and because each is already disposed to love the other; all they have to do is pluck up the courage to admit their feelings and to disregard external moral inhibition. The obstacles are few, so the narrative is relatively simple; the main interest of the play obviously lies elsewhere.

'Tis Pity She's a Whore is not so much about incest, then, as about a situation of which incest is a part – the part that happens to have most horrified, and therefore most preoccupied, many readers. One reason why it stands out is that, particularly in the early part of the action, Ford is careful to develop a sense of the sheer ordinariness of his Italian setting: the action takes place in a lived-in world, scarcely touched by the politics of state, and the

---

[29] Audrey Williamson, *Theatre of Two Decades* (London, 1951), p. 282; Peter Carthew, *Plays and Players* (October, 1961), p. 15; Paul Taylor, *The Independent,* 9 May 1992; Nicholas de Jongh, *Evening Standard,* 8 October 1999; Susannah Clapp, *The Observer,* 10 October 1999.

Suzan Sylvester as Annabella is reproached by Richard
Cordery's Friar Bonaventura, Act III, scene vi, Royal National
Theatre, 1988, directed by Alan Ayckbourn; Nobby
Clark/National Theatre

characters lead recognizable everyday lives in which domestic relationships between family members, and with servants, are paramount. They visit one another at home, hold dinner parties, and enjoy the arts: Philotis plays the lute, Soranzo reads and writes poetry, Bergetto loves visiting fairground attractions and puppet shows.[30] In production, directors who want to present the lovers as appealing innocents usually find they have to disregard Ford's emphasis and make Parma instead a highly-coloured environment of evil and corruption full of things that are nastier and more grotesque than anything in the original text: Roland Joffé's 1980 production for BBC television inserted a scene where Vasques anally rapes Hippolita, for example, and Philip Prowse's even more radically adapted version at Glasgow in 1988 portrayed Bergetto as a hunchbacked, mentally-handicapped mute whom his uncle (or father?) the Cardinal is trying to dispose of in marriage.[31] Though, as we shall see, the text's Parma does contain some dark undertones, there is no question of mitigating incest by any such crude contrast. Several successful twentieth-century productions updated the setting, thereby evading the misleading Gothic suggestions that can accompany period costume: audiences were left to focus on the familiar domestic detail, like (at the RSC in 1977) the lovers' frantic remaking of the bed in which they have just had sex, or (in the Actors' Company production of 1972) the brittle, civilized elegance of Soranzo's world, with its bone china, fine silver, evening dress, and – in the final scene – lots of white table-linen for the characters to bleed on. Some theatre critics worried over 'the problem of expressing Jacobean passions in white tie and tails' (as one put it apropos of the Actors' Company production), but the incongruity is entirely to the point.[32] Incest isn't allowed to be just the lesser social evil, venial in comparison with the horrors that surround it; productions which try to make it so simplify the play and draw much of its challenging sting.

At the hub of the plot lies the process of finding Annabella a husband, and this too was a commonplace social practice in the period, though one that is less recognizably so in productions with updated period settings. Renaissance daughters needed to become wives because fathers needed to transfer patriarchal responsibility to husbands: as Giovanni tells Annabella, albeit in jest, 'You must be married, mistress . . . Someone must have you.' (II.i.22–3) This meant that there had to be an acceptable financial

---

[30] For an extensive reading of the play in these terms, see Verna Foster, '*'Tis Pity She's a Whore* as City Tragedy' in Michael Neill (ed.), *John Ford: Critical Re-Visions* (Cambridge, 1988), pp. 181–200.

[31] Joffé's television production was transmitted on 7 May 1980; an archive recording exists at the BBC.

[32] Eric Shorter, *Daily Telegraph,* 6 September 1972.

settlement, but the daughter also had formally to consent to the match. There is nothing at all unusual about the way these negotiations are conducted in the play.[33] Money is an issue (it is clearly the rich booby Bergetto's only asset as a potential son-in-law), but unlike many a tyrannical stage father of the time, Florio genuinely cares about Annabella's happiness as well as her material well-being:

> As for worldly fortune,
> I am, I thank my stars, blessed with enough.
> My care is how to match her to her liking:
> I would not have her marry wealth, but love. (I.iii.8–11)

She is twice introduced to a suitor, first Bergetto in II.vi and then Soranzo in III.ii, and each time her father expressly gives her freedom to speak her mind, albeit in the latter case with a strong recommendation in Soranzo's favour. Whereas Shakespeare's Juliet is presented with a stark choice between marrying Paris or begging in the streets, and seeks Friar Laurence's help in finding a way out of the dilemma, the only excessive pressure on Annabella comes from the Friar and his alarming account of eternal torment, forcing her to a penitent acceptance of the husband Florio evidently wants for her.

One factor which complicates the play's sense of the mundane is its attention to the striations of social class among its characters. There are hints of this in the way they are formally addressed – Soranzo and the Cardinal are called 'Lord', Florio and Donado 'Signor', servants like Vasques by name alone – and many details point up particular class attitudes: the nobly born Hippolita's disdain for Annabella, 'Madam Merchant' (II.ii.48), who has supplanted her in Soranzo's affections; Florio's bourgeois respect for religion and learning in the person of the Friar, 'A man made up of holiness' (II.vi.4); Vasques' below-stairs devotion to proverbial folk wisdom. But the things which most repeatedly divide them along class lines are sex and violence.

Bad behaviour is not uncommon in Ford's Parma, but it is also not endemic. The servants are sometimes casually coarse, notably Annabella's tutoress Putana, whose sole criterion for a desirable fiancé is sexual prowess. Productions often emphasize this side of the role by portraying her as a frustrated older woman, mutton dressing herself as lamb: the blonde hair of Annette Badland's 1999 Young Vic Putana rather obviously came from a

---

[33] For a detailed account of marriage settlement procedures in the period see Ann Jennalie Cook, *Making a Match: Courtship in Shakespeare and his Society* (Princeton, 1991).

dye bottle, and in David Leveaux's 1991 RSC production, Sheila Reid's version had pathetically tarted herself up in black silk lingerie and suspenders; many a Vasques has wormed the truth out of many a Putana in IV.iii by using physical intimacy ranging in degree from a comforting cuddle to outright masturbation. It is appropriate that the servants are the ones who most abet their masters' sexual misconduct, Vasques in helping Soranzo to evade the consequences of his illicit affair with Hippolita, and Putana in being the lovers' only secular confidante.

What distinguishes the aristocrats, meanwhile, is a privileged insouciance in the way they treat people who get in the way of their desires and objectives. It is striking that this seems to become more calculating as matters escalate: Hippolita initially tries to promote her extra-marital affair not by having her husband murdered but by encouraging him to undertake a dangerous journey and merely hoping that it will be the death of him, and Grimaldi's first attempts to beat Soranzo in the marriage game use slander rather than the sword; in both cases, elaborate revenge plots only come later. Until the final scenes, all of the play's physical violence arises from upper class vindictiveness and in-fighting, and the participants evidently do not much care what happens to innocent bystanders like Bergetto, killed when Grimaldi mistakes him for Soranzo in the dark. This is a moment at which audiences usually see the unbearable pity of it (a reviewer of the 1923 Phoenix Society production even found 'dazzling psychological truth' in Harold Scott's terrified, dying Bergetto);[34] but it is typical of the aristocratic characters' behaviour that the Cardinal's response to the crime should be one of class solidarity: Grimaldi is granted protection for no better reason than that 'He is no common man, but nobly born / Of princes' blood' (III.ix.56–7).

Among the middle classes, though, other standards obtain. The structural spine of the play is a sequence of social meals, each one interrupted by violence: the off-stage lunch which Florio holds for the suitors, during which a fight breaks out between Grimaldi and Vasques, the latter acting for Soranzo (I.ii); the wedding feast, at which Hippolita plans to poison Soranzo but is double-crossed by Vasques (IV.i); and Soranzo's birthday feast, when his dark plot involving hired banditti is pre-empted by Giovanni (V.vi). On each occasion, Florio's reaction is revealing. First he is clearly distressed at the degree of ill feeling among the competing suitors at his table:

> I would not for my wealth my daughter's love
> Should cause the spilling of one drop of blood. (I.ii.60–1)

[34] M.A., *The Spectator*, 3 February 1923.

After blood is metaphorically shed at the second meal when Hippolita dies by her own poison, he is the first person to speak, stigmatizing her as uniquely, incredibly horrible: 'Was e'er so vile a creature?' (IV.i.99) Thus he draws an insulating distinction between this extreme event and the norms of his own life: there is no expectation that he will ever see its like again. When he does, at the third meal, he rises to full-scale denial: Giovanni's entrance with a freshly eviscerated human heart impaled on his dagger is explicable only as madness, and his admission of incest simply cannot be true – 'his rage belies him!' (V.vi.51) This is middle-class propriety facing the dangerous edge of things, and capable of no adequate response; it should be no great surprise that moments later Florio dies of shock.

This attention to rank and, at Florio's level, to proper social demeanour, means that deviant behaviour stands out. The obvious example is Bergetto, Donado's nephew, who is characterized as juvenile beneath his years. Though of marriageable age, he is sexually innocent: he seems to know that visiting prostitutes is the done thing among gallants, but he has evidently never used one himself, for he wildly overestimates the fee (II.vi. 107–8), and later he doesn't understand the 'monstrous swelling' (III.v.45) he gets when he kisses Philotis. He is also still subject to corporal punishment, as Poggio reminds him (II.iv.44), and apparently not unused to babyish incontinence: when Grimaldi runs him through in the dark, he is puzzled that this time the obvious explanation for finding his clothes wet doesn't fit – 'I am sure I cannot piss forward and backward, and yet I am wet before and behind.' (III.vii. 11–12) He lacks the maturity or sophistication to conform to the polite standards of middle-class society, a point which is enhanced when Poggio is played, as Guy Henry portrayed him at the RSC in 1991, as his more intelligent minder.

There are many prominent instances of Bergetto's irrepressible gaucherie of behaviour and even of language. Most of the characters' dialogue is notable for its restraint: Giovanni will not name the female genitalia ('what is ... for pleasure framed' (II.v.57)), Putana avoids referring directly to menstruation (III.iii.12–13), and almost everyone typically speaks of 'Heaven' or uses some other genteel periphrasis for the name of God. Bergetto is the first to swear (and Vasques is the only other), using one of the most offensive oaths, ''Sfoot' (III.i.4). As the play's principal broad-comedy role, he inhabits a different dimension from the rest of the cast: he owes his dramatic pedigree more to Jonsonian comic twits like Bartholomew Cokes in *Bartholomew Fair* (1614) than to the play's dominant strains of philosophical tragedy and social realism, and in production the part offers actors exceptional latitude of interpretation. Richard Bonneville's Woosterish version in the 1991 RSC production approached life with asinine seriousness, and other actors have seized the opportunity for slapstick. Played as a 'queenly fop' by John Tordoff in the 1972 Actors' Company production, for example, Bergetto licked away at an ice cream which eventually plopped onto another character's polished shoe: the moment neatly underlined the character's misplacement in Parma's smooth, cultured society, here a genteel Italy of the early 1900s.[35] The character is also sometimes made physically distinct by casting an unusually tall actor, like Stephen Thorne at the Mermaid Theatre in 1961, or by making him excessively fat or thin: the National Theatre's first Bergetto, in 1972, was the lanky David Bradley, followed by a podgy Russell Dixon in 1988, who looked in his crimson satin cavalier suit more like an overdressed King Charles spaniel than a human being.

People also stand out because they are strangers in town. Parma is portrayed as a close society whose members have, at least within their own class, the kind of easy intimacy with one another that we see when Florio comforts the grieving Donado in the aftermath of Bergetto's murder. So it is noticed when, for example, a new physician arrives, as he says, from Padua: his medical ability 'through the city / Is freely talked of' (II.iii.35–6), but nobody really knows him as a person because he is still in the early stages of establishing himself socially (and, of course, because he is really Richardetto in disguise). We can see the same process behind the way, after the murder, an officer gropes around his memory for the identity of the person he saw running through the streets with a bloodstained rapier: 'sure I know the man, they say a is a soldier. [*To* FLORIO] He that loved your daughter, sir' (III.ix.17–18). Grimaldi is a Roman who has come to Parma recently: the officer has seen him around, and has heard the common talk about his occupation and the purpose of his visit, but little more, and certainly not his name.

Rumour and gossip – 'the speech of the people' (II.i.47), as Putana calls it – run through the homely world of *'Tis Pity She's a Whore*. As well as outsiders, the Parmesans talk about scandalous behaviour amongst their own: Hippolita's brazenly open affair with Soranzo is widely known (Putana takes it as evidence that Soranzo is the most suitable of Annabella's suitors), and later the breakdown of his marriage is a matter of common report; 'Much talk I hear' (IV.ii.13), says Richardetto. And there are good reputations, too: in the second act, Annabella is told,

> Loud fame in large report hath spoke your praise
> As well for virtue as perfection. (II.i.59–60)

Only minutes before, however, she was talking about having lost her virginity to her brother.

---

[35] Nicholas de Jongh, *The Guardian*, 6 September 1972.

Gossip, carefully drawn out of Putana by Vasques in IV.iii, is the way the incest ultimately comes to light, but before then the play is shot through with double meaning and dramatic irony: sex between brother and sister is a possibility which seems literally unthinkable, so that characters misinterpret events and behaviour, ascribing meanings which are often the polar opposite of the truth. Florio's paternal attitude to Giovanni is one of mixed pride and concern: he expects his studies will 'teach him how to gain another world' (II. vi.5), but also worries that being 'so devoted to his book' (I.iii.5) will make him ill; whereas in reality Giovanni's mastery of academic argument enables him to pursue bodily desires at the expense of his spiritual health. He is universally regarded as the one young man who can safely be left unchaperoned with Annabella (even Putana thinks so at first, and says she would expect a bribe from anyone else), when actually he is the only sexual partner she wants; their father sees nothing wrong in his wearing a ring which, by the terms of their dead mother's will, Annabella may give only to her husband (II.vi.36–42). And when she falls pregnant, morning sickness is diagnosed as 'a fullness of her blood' (III.iv.8), a condition suffered only by young female virgins: it is the starkest possible illustration of the way false assumptions shape the other characters' understanding of the situation and so keep incest hidden from a gossipy outside world where there are few other secrets.

Another element of society which needs to be considered here is the Church. With its Friar and Cardinal, the play has an overtly Roman Catholic setting: productions often emphasize this with supplementary trappings like the overpowering smell of incense which filled the Glasgow Citizens' Theatre in 1988, or the large crucifix which dominated the 1977 RSC stage design. Ford's England, in contrast, was a broadly Protestant country, for all that Queen Henrietta Maria, the original acting company's patron, had blurred the ideological lines at court by introducing a fashionable Catholic coterie. The play's narrative contains a thread of suspicion about the institutions of the Catholic church, which is most explicitly focused on the Cardinal who abuses his power for purposes which are far from spiritual: the characters express open outrage when he shelters the murderer Grimaldi (Guy Henry's Poggio removed the crucifix from his neck, threw it to the floor, and spat on it in a powerful moment immediately before the interval), and I have never seen a performance where his closing confiscation of 'all the gold and jewels' (V.vi.148) was not met with a sardonic laugh from the audience; his pragmatic materialism need not be represented as corrupt (though it often is) for it to be obviously inappropriate in a churchman. But if Friar Bonaventura is clearly a more sincere Christian, he too is a focus for criticism.

Giovanni may make himself 'poor of secrets' (I.i.15) when he tells the Friar about his incestuous desires, but all he is really doing is marginally

The crucifix dominating the set of the 1977 Royal Shakespeare
Company production directed by Ron Daniels, with Simon
Rouse as Giovanni confessing to Matthew Guinness as the
Friar; Joe Cocks Studio Collection,
© Shakespeare Birthplace Trust

widening a privileged circle of knowledge. One of the practices attacked in anti-Catholic writing of the period was confidential confession, which put priests in possession of sensitive personal information, but also prevented them from divulging it; this was thought to make them accessories, albeit perhaps unwillingly, in all manner of crime and immorality which could be restrained or punished if it were only known about. This is precisely Bonaventura's position: as confessor to both Giovanni and Annabella, he knows of their incest but can only counsel repentance, not tell anyone. How difficult he finds this dilemma is a matter for interpretation in performance, but it is striking that his practical advice always involves secrecy. Giovanni is encouraged to repent and pray for grace, but to do it in strict privacy:

> lock thee fast
> Alone within thy chamber, then fall down
> On both thy knees, and grovel on the ground.　(I.i.69–71)

Similarly, after he has pressurized Annabella into penitence, there is no question of telling even those, such as Florio, who arguably have a right to know:

> 'Tis thus agreed:
> First, for your honour's safety, that you marry
> The Lord Soranzo; next, to save your soul,
> Leave off this life, and henceforth live to him.　(III.vi.35–8)

The concern for her soul may be conscientious, but why should he be interested in her honour? It is not as if there is no alternative course of action available. The play juxtaposes Annabella's unusual romantic life with the more straightforward love story of Richardetto's niece Philotis, who is introduced as a virgin (II.i.62) just after Annabella has ceased to be one, who experiences sexual awakening when she kisses Bergetto (III.v.37), and who is finally packed off to the chaste life of a nun after her fiancé's murder. If, as Richardetto says, 'No life is blessèd but the way to heaven' (IV.ii.21), then it would be entirely proper for Annabella to follow the same route. In his complementary concern for her worldly well-being, the Friar only participates in the hypocrisy surrounding honour, where what matters most is not being found out. It is a bad mistake, and not just because it neglects other legitimate interests: Soranzo is bound eventually to find out (the pregnancy is so far advanced before the marriage that there can be no question of his being responsible), and from there the plot winds out to its catastrophe.

SECRETS AND MORTALITY

The central dynamic of the play's narrative is the discovery of secrets, but some secrets are better kept than others. We are made privy to the incest throughout its development, but other characters' behaviour is sinister because it is not fully explained. Vasques is a case in point: we are left pondering the unusually proactive role he takes in furthering Hippolita's and Soranzo's plots until he finally explains his motivation as a bizarrely ethical sense of loyalty to his master's family.[36] In other cases, notably Richardetto, we are never told at all: he will not take Philotis into his confidence (II.iii.16) and, hoping to resume his place in society, he has too much to lose from a full confession at the end; all we see of his revenge are its collateral effects, not the plan behind them. But the most important hidden agenda is Lord Soranzo's in the final act.

We are shown the preparations leading up to the birthday feast, including the engagement of banditti who are given a watchword for action; we hear Annabella tell Giovanni, 'there's but a dining-time / 'Twixt us and our confusion' (V.v.17–18); but we never see the plot come to its intended fruition because Giovanni seizes the initiative. Obviously one of Soranzo's objectives is a revenge killing of Giovanni (and possibly the rest of his immediate family) in the presence of the eminent men, 'The states of Parma' (V.ii.19), who are the other guests. The public nature of the act is important because it demands a strong element of justification: even aristocratic dinner parties are not normally enlivened by blood-letting, but last time, after publicly murdering Hippolita, Vasques was exonerated and called 'a trusty servant' (IV.i.101) because he could show good cause for it. The crucial detail on this occasion is Soranzo's instruction that Annabella should 'deck herself in all her bridal robes' (V.ii.11): there is more to this than the poignant ominousness of Desdemona's wedding sheets in *Othello*, as we can see in performance if Annabella is already dressed when she next appears in V.v. Ford makes Giovanni very explicit about how long his relationship with her lasted:

> For nine months' space in secret I enjoyed
> Sweet Annabella's sheets; nine months I lived
> A happy monarch of her heart and her.   (V.vi.43–5)

If we take this to indicate that her pregnancy is close to full term, and therefore visible, then Soranzo's intentions are clear: the murder is to be preceded, and sanctioned, by a public shaming ritual which will lay open what

---

[36] For a fuller account, see Martin Wiggins, *Journeymen in Murder: The Assassin in English Renaissance Drama* (Oxford, 1991), pp. 193–5.

was previously hidden, and unsuspected; Annabella will be exposed in her wedding dress as the pregnant bride she was, damaged goods returned to the merchant 'in the original packaging', a living emblem of her own whoredom.[37]

This makes an instructive contrast with what actually happens in the final scene when Giovanni makes his first, and only, open intervention in the play's social action. Soranzo's plot has a certain rigid propriety in its use of a convivial occasion to reveal and punish deeds offensive to Parma's prevailing social mores. Giovanni's supervening action – his entrance with Annabella's heart spitted on his dagger – has an appalling impropriety which he intensifies when he regales the seated diners with talk of food:

> You came to feast, my lords, with dainty fare.
> I came to feast too, but I digged for food
> In a much richer mine than gold or stone
> Of any value balanced. 'Tis a heart.   (V.vi.23–6)

It too is a stage image that literally reveals to view what was hitherto hidden, an internal organ of the body, by making an emblem of it. Throughout the play, the heart has been rhetorically established as the seat of love; hence it is, he says, 'A heart . . . in which is mine entombed' (V.vi.27). Pierced, it can also signify the pains or cruelty of love, and several of its different valencies – the phallic knife piercing the vaginal heart, for example, or the killing of love – can be taken together to exemplify more particularly Giovanni's role, not himself the tragic hero but the agent of destruction at all the key stages of his sister's tragedy: he whores her, he impregnates her, and at last he kills her, eliciting a cry of 'Brother, unkind, unkind' (V.v.93). Annabella's heart assaults us with a range of possible significances, in contrast with the simple clear statement in the spectacle Soranzo aimed to orchestrate.[38] Yet ultimately it is as pointless trying to read a coded meaning here as it is to agonize over whether the play promotes or condemns incest.

Tragedy is not a genre which trades in definitive meaning. It shows how things fall apart into chaos and entropy, and the survivors' closing attempts

---

[37] Ford may once again have been thinking of an old play by Marston, *Antonio's Revenge* (1600), in which the tyrant Piero orders, 'Produce the strumpet in her bridal robes, / That she may blush t' appear so white in show / And black in inward substance.' (IV.i.81–3).

[38] The most thorough and informed attempt to read the iconography of the heart is made by Michael Neill, '"What Strange Riddle's This?": Deciphering *'Tis Pity She's a Whore*', in Michael Neill (ed.), *John Ford: Critical Re-Visions* (Cambridge, 1988), pp. 153–79.

to 'restore order' are always unsatisfying, or compromised; so it is misguided to look for some stable way of reading and making 'acceptable' the extreme events which have gone before. We cannot expect to be able to say, with the Cardinal, ''Tis pity she's a whore' (V.vi.159) and leave the theatre confident in the victory of society over incestuous deviance, any more than we should feel secure in identifying finally with Giovanni. In the image of the eviscerated heart, there is a collision between an enormous metaphoric suggestiveness and a concrete reality that resists interpretation, which was anticipated in Annabella's mockingly literal misconstruction of Soranzo's conventional love rhetoric:

> SORANZO
> Did you but see my heart, then would you swear –
> ANNABELLA
> That you were dead.   (III.ii.24–5)

There is a difference between the metaphor and the reality, between an emblematic picture of a heart and the grisly human organ itself: if there is something bathetic about the legendary (and perhaps apocryphal) programme credit, 'heart by Dewhurst the Family Butcher', there is also something utterly to the point. We may struggle to find an answer to its 'strange riddle' (V.vi.29), to make the image discursive, transcendent, beyond the merely physical; but in the theatre our efforts will always founder on that very physicality, confounded by the terrible fascination of a piece of meat.

Florio's response is twice to call his son a madman, but for us to follow suit would be intellectually lazy. Giovanni's actions in the crescendo of the play are not inexplicable: it is a mistake to attribute to him the opacity of meaning that is a characteristic of the stage image he creates. By the fifth act, the world-shaping exercise of intellect has liberated in him a tremendous will to power, which responds to danger by offering destruction for destruction:

> If I must totter like a well-grown oak,
> Some under-shrubs shall in my weighty fall
> Be crushed to splits; with me they all shall perish.   (V.iii.77–9)

To an extent, too, he acts from that pagan sense of honour which also motivates the doomed Brutus in *Julius Caesar* when, beaten by his enemies to the pit, he adjudges it more worthy to leap in of his own volition; so Giovanni, certain of his own fall, takes it upon himself so that it may be his triumph and not his enemy's. As Antonin Artaud put it in 1933, he 'places himself above retribution and crime by a kind of indescribably passionate crime, places himself above threats, above horror by an even greater horror that baffles both law and morals and those who dare to set themselves up as judges.'[39] It is through this assertion of existential superiority that the stage action is moved beyond discourse and into the visceral atrocity celebrated by Artaud as the theatre of cruelty – a savage spectacle which disrupts the cultural norms and expectations onto which it obtrudes. Foreshadowed throughout the play from the point in I.ii when Giovanni offers Annabella his dagger and invites her to inspect his heart, this climax is where the play's curiously bifurcated structure finally pays off: it is for this moment that Giovanni has been kept back, linked to the rest of the action only through the hinge of Annabella while the play developed its separate social world of bourgeois ambition and aristocratic love and honour. When the two worlds intersect and the play's secret parts are exposed to view, all the easy certainties of everyday life dissolve, and its petty forms of social organization become irrelevant. The ultimate truth embodied in Annabella's heart is not what we strive to make it, but the very corporeal meatiness that we would rather evade: it forcefully confronts us with what tragedy always asserts, and what our pretensions to civilization and culture are so keen to deny – the pitiful, terrible frailty of our mortal lives.

NOTE ON THE TEXT

The control-text for any modern edition of *'Tis Pity She's a Whore* is inevitably the Quarto of 1633 (Q) printed by Nicholas Okes for Richard Collins. Since it contains a dedication signed by Ford, it is generally taken to be an authorized edition printed from an authorial manuscript. The play was not reprinted in the seventeenth century, although in 1652 a copy of Q was bound with six other Ford Quartos, with a general printed title page, to produce a collection of Ford's *Comedies, tragi-comedies; & tragaedies*.[40] All subsequent editions derive their text either directly or indirectly from Q.

Q is a book rich in bibliographical interest, providing much material for speculation about printing-house mishaps and even a visit to the press by

---

[39] Antonin Artaud, 'Theatre and the Plague', in *Collected Works*, tr. Victor Corti (London, 1968–), iv. 18.

[40] The volume is now held by the National Library of Scotland. The collection was originally owned by the seventeenth-century antiquary Walter Chetwynd of Ingestre, Staffordshire (or possibly his father, also named Walter; Walter junior, who died in 1693, would have been no more than nineteen years old in 1652).

the author.[41] However, there is little to pose any major textual difficulty: a few words are misprinted and verse and prose are often confused or mislined (sometimes because the copy was wrongly marked up into pages, forcing the compositor to squash and stretch material to fit the space available). A number of surviving copies contain sheets printed after press-correction, which introduce a total of forty-five variants; in this edition the corrected reading has been silently adopted in all substantive instances. The notes record all emendations and significant changes to the lineation of verse passages (including prose erroneously set as verse in Q); but changes to the division of prose passages and verse lines split to accommodate them within the margins of the Q page are not recorded. Q divides the text into five acts, and I have followed the usual convention of marking a new scene every time the stage is completely cleared. Q supplies a list of 'The Actors' Names', which provides some interesting hints about how Ford conceived the characters and their relationships, but which requires interpretation and, obviously, does not address itself to the needs of the modern reader; in this edition the list of the persons of the play has been compiled afresh, while the 1633 list appears as an appendix.

Speech prefixes have been silently expanded and all Latin stage directions silently translated into English, with the exception of the now-conventional *exit* and *exeunt*. Although it is possible that some of Q's stage directions were written for the seventeenth-century reader rather than for the playhouse, there are a number of points where necessary stage action is unclear, or where the reader is obliged to infer actions from subsequent dialogue references to them; stage directions (or parts thereof) which appear in square brackets have been added to resolve such issues. A number of directions to enter are given late in Q, presumably to indicate the point at which the characters concerned enter the action, rather than the stage; with one problematic exception (on which, see the note to II.iii.28 s.d.), such stage directions are repositioned in this edition to indicate the point at which those characters become visible to a theatre audience, and to other characters already on stage.

Spelling and punctuation are modernized throughout in accordance with New Mermaid series conventions. No previous editor has attempted a full modernization of Q's light, rhetorical punctuation, which is eccentric (and sometimes mystifying) in its use of dashes, and tends to use commas and semi-colons to separate entirely distinct syntactic units. This edition uses heavier, grammatical punctuation in an effort to guide the reader through the syntax.

---

[41] For a full account of Q's printing, see Roper, pp. lxiii–lxviii.

Perhaps the greatest challenge which the play offers its editor lies in the deceptive simplicity of some of its language: a number of its unadorned and unspecific lines are open to irreconcilable alternative interpretations. This is quite a different matter from the deliberate, meaningful ambiguity celebrated by the critical school of William Empson (and which is also present in some parts of the play), where the multiple senses of a word coexist and interact to create a richer matrix of significance; I refer instead to cases which might be seen as the literary equivalent of Schrodinger's cat, where the process of realizing the text forces you to choose one meaning and exclude all others. The less virtual the play becomes, the more these possibilities will cease to exist: an edition with modernized spelling and (especially) punctuation will have closed down some, and a production all of them. In preparing this edition, I have tried to be alert to this issue, to avoid imposing one possible stage realization at the expense of another, and to discuss the more clear-cut interpretative options in the notes.

Like all editors, I owe much to the work of my predecessors. After Q, the play next appeared in print as part of Robert Dodsley's *Select Collection of Old Plays* (1744), which was later revised by Isaac Reed in 1780. From Dodsley onwards, the editorial history has been one of progressively introducing emendations to Q, and more recently rejecting them in favour of the original Q readings; this edition continues the latter trend. I have been especially indebted to the important contributions to the play's bibliographical and textual history in the editions of N. W. Bawcutt (1966) and Derek Roper (1975), and to the thorough modernization of the spelling in that of Marion Lomax (1995). I have also found useful the editions of Henry William Weber (1811), William Gifford (1827), Alexander Dyce (1869), A. K. McIlwraith (1953), Brian Morris (1968), Keith Sturgess (1970), Colin Gibson (1986), and Simon Barker (1997).

ABBREVIATIONS

EDITIONS OF THE PLAY CITED

Barker   *'Tis Pity She's a Whore,* ed. Simon Barker, Routledge English Texts (London, 1997)

Dodsley   Robert Dodsley (ed.), *A Select Collection of Old Plays* (London, 1744)

Dyce   *The Works of John Ford,* ed. William Gifford, rev. Alexander Dyce (London, 1869), vol. 1

Gibson   *The Selected Plays of John Ford,* ed. Colin Gibson (Cambridge, 1986)

Gifford   *The Dramatic Works of John Ford,* ed. William Gifford (London, 1827), vol. 1

Lomax   *'Tis Pity She's a Whore and Other Plays,* ed. Marion Lomax, Oxford English Drama (Oxford, 1995)

McIlwraith   *Five Stuart Tragedies,* ed. A. K. McIlwraith (London, 1953)

Morris   *'Tis Pity She's a Whore,* ed. Brian Morris, The New Mermaids 1st edition (London, 1968)

Q   The Quarto of 1633

Roper   *'Tis Pity She's a Whore,* ed. Derek Roper, The Revels Plays (London, 1975)

Schmitz   'A Critical Edition of John Ford's *'Tis Pitty Shee's a Whore',* ed. Elsie Kemp Schmitz (unpublished Cambridge M.Litt. thesis, 1959)

Sturgess   *Three Plays,* ed. Keith Sturgess (Harmondsworth, 1970)

Weber   *The Dramatic Works of John Ford,* ed. Henry William Weber (Edinburgh, 1811), vol. 1

OTHER WORKS

First Fruits   John Florio, *Florio His First Fruites* (London, 1578)

N&Q   *Notes and Queries*

OED   *The Oxford English Dictionary,* 2nd edn, ed. J. A. Simpson and E. S. C. Weiner (Oxford, 1989)

Tilley   Morris Palmer Tilley, *A Dictionary of the Proverbs in England in the Sixteenth and Seventeenth Centuries* (Ann Arbor, Mich., 1950)

World   John Florio, *A Worlde of Wordes* (London, 1598)

Other plays of Ford are quoted from the following editions: *The Broken Heart*, ed. T. J. B. Spencer (Manchester, 1980); *The Fancies, Chaste and Noble*, ed. Dominick J. Hart (New York and London, 1985); *The Sun's Darling*, in *The Dramatic Works of Thomas Dekker*, ed. Fredson Bowers, (Cambridge, 1953–61). Shakespeare is quoted from *The Complete Works*, ed. Stanley Wells, Gary Taylor, John Jowett, and William Montgomery (Oxford, 1986), and the Bible from the King James translation of 1611. Other editions cited are: William Barksted and Lewis Machin, *The Insatiate Countess*, in *Four Jacobean Sex Tragedies*, ed. Martin Wiggins (Oxford, 1998); Lording Barry, *Ram Alley*, ed. Peter Corbin and Douglas Sedge (Nottingham, 1981); Thomas Dekker, *The Noble Spanish Soldier*, in *The Dramatic Works*, ed. Bowers; John Marston, *'The Malcontent' and Other Plays*, ed. Keith Sturgess, Oxford English Drama (Oxford, 1997); John Webster, *The Duchess of Malfi*, ed. Elizabeth M. Brennan (London, 1993); and *The Fatal Marriage*, ed. S. Brigid Younghughes and Harold Jenkins (Oxford, 1959 for 1958).

In the footnotes to the text:
     ed.   this edition
     s.d   stage direction
     s.p   speech prefix

FURTHER READING

Anderson, Donald K., jun. (ed.), *'Concord in Discord': The Plays of John Ford, 1586–1986* (New York, 1986)

Brooke, Nicholas, *Horrid Laughter in Jacobean Tragedy* (London, 1979)

Champion, Larry S., 'Ford's *'Tis Pity She's a Whore* and the Jacobean Tragic Perspective', *PMLA* 90 (1975), 78–87

Clark, Ira, *Professional Playwrights: Massinger, Ford, Shirley, and Brome* (Lexington, 1992)

Clerico, Terri, 'The Politics of Blood: John Ford's *'Tis Pity She's a Whore*', *English Literary Renaissance* 22 (1992), 405–34

Farr, Dorothy M., *John Ford and the Caroline Theatre* (London and Basingstoke, 1979)

Hopkins, Lisa, *John Ford's Political Theatre* (Manchester, 1994)

Hoy, Cyrus, 'Ignorance in Knowledge: Marlowe's Faustus and Ford's Giovanni', *Modern Philology* 57 (1960), 145–54

Huebert, Ronald, *John Ford: Baroque English Dramatist* (Montreal and London, 1977)

Leech, Clifford, *John Ford and the Drama of His Time* (London, 1957)

Lomax, Marion, *Stage Images and Traditions: Shakespeare to Ford* (Cambridge, 1987)

McCabe, Richard A., *Incest, Drama, and Nature's Law, 1550–1700* (Cambridge, 1993)

Neill, Michael (ed.), *John Ford: Critical Re-Visions* (Cambridge, 1988)

Oliver, H. J., *The Problem of John Ford* (Melbourne, London, and New York, 1955)

Rosen, Carol C., 'The Language of Cruelty in Ford's *'Tis Pity She's a Whore*', *Comparative Drama* 8 (1974), 356–68

Stavig, Mark, *John Ford and the Traditional Moral Order* (Madison and London, 1968)

Wymer, Rowland, *Webster and Ford* (London, 1995)

Information about recent productions, including photographs, is available in a variety of locations scattered across the internet. Readers need to bear in mind that websites are not always reliable sources of scholarly information, and that they are often transient; currently available sites can be found using most standard search engines.

MAJOR BRITISH PRODUCTIONS
IN THE TWENTIETH CENTURY

1923   The Phoenix Society at the Shaftesbury Theatre, London
       Cast: Moyna MacGill (Annabella); Ion Swinley (Giovanni); Henry
       Oscar (Soranzo); Harold Scott (Bergetto)
       Director: Alan Wade

1934–5   The Arts Theatre Club, London
       Cast: Selma Vaz Dias (Annabella); Terence de Marney (Giovanni);
       Neil Porter (Soranzo); Norman Shelley (Vasques); Mark Dignam
       (Donado); Harold Scott (Bergetto); Walter Fitzgerald (Richard-
       etto)
       Director: Harold Mortlake

1940–1   Cambridge Arts Theatre (later transferred to the Strand Theatre,
       London)
       Cast: Rosalind Iden (Annabella); Donald Wolfit (Giovanni); Hubert
       Langley (Soranzo); Reginald Jarman (Vasques) (H. Worrall-
       Thompson later took over the role); Michael Ashwin (Bergetto);
       Richard Wordsworth (Cardinal)
       Director: Donald Wolfit

1953   BBC radio production, broadcast 30 August
       Director: Martyn C. Webster

1955   Nottingham Playhouse

1958   Cambridge A.D.C. at the Cambridge Arts Theatre
       Cast: Margaret Drabble (Annabella); Richard Marquand (Gio-
       vanni); Eleanor Bron (Putana); Derek Jacobi (Soranzo); Clive Swift
       (Vasques); Richard Cottrell (Bergetto)
       Directors: Elsie Kemp and Richard Cottrell

1961   Mermaid Theatre, London
       Cast: Zena Walker (Annabella); Edward de Souza (Giovanni);
       Patience. Collier (Putana); David Sumner (Soranzo); John Wood-
       vine (Vasques); Stephen Thorne (Bergetto); Jeremy Geidt (Poggio)
       Director: David Thompson

1962   BBC radio production, broadcast 29 June
       Director: Martyn C. Webster

1968   Bristol Old Vic
       Director: John David

1970   BBC radio production, broadcast 16 January
       Director: John Tydeman

1972–4   The Actors' Company and the Cambridge Theatre Company

Cast: Felicity Kendall (Annabella) (Paola Dionisotti later took over the role); Ian McKellen (Giovanni); Frank Middlemass (Florio); Robert Eddison (Friar); Edward Petherbridge (Soranzo); Jack Shepherd (Vasques) (John Bennett later took over the role); Tenniel Evans (Donado); John Tordoff (Bergetto)
Director: David Giles

1972 National Theatre Touring Company
Cast: Anna Carteret (Annabella); Nicholas Clay (Giovanni); James Hayes (Putana); Gawn Grainger (Vasques); David Bradley (Bergetto); Diana Rigg (Hippolita)
Director: Roland Joffé

1973 Film version adapted by Giuseppe Patroni Griffi
Cast: Charlotte Rampling (Annabella); Oliver Tobias (Giovanni); Antonio Falsi (Friar); Fabio Testi (Soranzo)
Director: Giuseppe Patroni Griffi

1977 Royal Shakespeare Company at the Other Place, Stratford-upon-Avon (later transferred to the Donmar Warehouse, London)
Cast: Barbara Kellerman (Annabella); Simon Rouse (Giovanni); Nigel Terry Soranzo); Geoffrey Hutchings (Vasques); Tim Wylton (Bergetto); Ron Cook (Poggio)
Director: Ron Daniels

1978 Northcott Theatre, Exeter
Director: Richard Digby Day

1980 BBC television version adapted by Richard Broke, Roland Joffé, and Kenneth McLeish; broadcast 7 May
Cast: Cherie Lunghi (Annabella); Kenneth Cranham (Giovanni); Colin Douglas (Florio); Tim Pigott-Smith (Vasques); Rodney Bewes (Bergetto)
Director: Roland Joffé

1980 New Theatre Company, at Theatrespace (later transferred to the Old Half Moon Theatre, London)
Director: Declan Donnellan

1988 Glasgow Citizens' Theatre
Cast: Yolanda Vasquez (Annabella); Tristram Wymark (Giovanni); Fidelis organ (Putana); Ron Donachie (Soranzo); Rupert Farley (Vasques)
Director: Philip Prowse

1988 Royal National Theatre, London
Cast: Suzan Sylvester (Annabella); Rupert Graves (Giovanni); Richard Cordery (Friar); Michael Simkins (Soranzo); Clive Francis (Vasques); Russell Dixon (Bergetto); Jim Barclay (Poggio)

Director: Alan Ayckbourn

1991–2 Royal Shakespeare Company at the Swan, Stratford-upon-Avon
(later transferred the Pit, London)
Cast: Saskia Reeves (Annabella); Jonathan Cullen (Giovanni);
Sheila Reid (Putana); Jonathan Newth (Friar); Tim McInnerny
(Soranzo); Jonathan Hyde (Vasques);Richard Bonneville (Bergetto);
Guy Henry (Poggio); Terence Wilton (Richardetto)
Director: David Leveaux

1995 Talawa Theatre Company, at the Lyric Studio, London
Cast: Ginny Holder (Annabella); Stephen Persaud (Giovanni);
Alan Igbon (Soranzo); Don Warrington (Vasques); Simon Clay-
ton (Bergetto)
Director: Yvonne Brewster

1999 Young Vic, London
Cast: Eve Best (Annabella); Jude Law (Giovanni); David Lyon (Flo-
rio); Annette Badland (Putana); Kevin McKidd; (Soranzo); Philip
Whitchurch (Vasques); Caroline Langrishe (Hippolita); Cather-
ine Bailey (Philotis)
Director: David Lan

NGLISH DEPARTMENT
VARLINGHAM SCHOOL

Quarto title page, 1633
By permission of the Master and Fellows of St John's College,
Cambridge

TIS
Pitty Shee's a Whore

Acted by the *Queenes* Maiesties Ser-
uants, at *The Phœnix* in
Drury-Lane.

LONDON.
Printed by *Nicholas Okes* for *Richard
Collins,* and are to be sold at his shop
in *Pauls* Church-yard, at the signe
of the three Kings. 1633.

[COMMENDATORY VERSE]

To my Friend, the Author.

With admiration I beheld this Whore
Adorned with beauty, such as might restore
(If ever being as thy Muse hath famed)
Her Giovanni, in his love unblamed.
The ready Graces lent their willing aid;   5
Pallas herself now played the chambermaid
And helped to put her dressings on: secure
Rest thou, that thy name herein shall endure
To th' end of age; and Annabella be
Gloriously fair, even in her infamy.   10

THOMAS ELLICE.

This does not appear in all copies of Q
5 *The . . . Graces* in classical mythology, the three daughters of Jupiter, who both personi-
fied and bestowed beauty and charm
6 *Pallas* surname of Athena, classical goddess of wisdom
11 THOMAS ELLICE born in 1607, a member of Gray's Inn from 1626 and, along with his elder
brother, Robert, a member of Ford's literary circle; see Mary Hobbs, 'Robert and Thomas
Ellice, Friends of Ford and Davenant', *N&Q* NS 21 (1974), 292–3

[DEDICATORY EPISTLE]

To the truly noble, John, Earl of Peterborough,
Lord Mordaunt, Baron of Turvey.

My Lord,

    Where a truth of merit hath a general warrant, there love is but a
debt, acknowledgment a justice. Greatness cannot often claim virtue   5
by inheritance; yet in this yours appears most eminent, for that you
are not more rightly heir to your fortunes, than glory shall be to your
memory. Sweetness of disposition ennobles a freedom of birth; in
both, your lawful interest adds honour to your own name, and mercy
to my presumption. Your noble allowance of these first fruits of my   10
leisure in the action, emboldens my confidence of your as noble construction in this presentment; especially since my service must ever
owe particular duty to your favours, by a particular engagement. The
gravity of the subject may easily excuse the lightness of the title; otherwise I had been a severe judge against mine own guilt. Princes have   15
vouchsafed grace to trifles, offered from a purity of devotion; your
lordship may likewise please to admit into your good opinion, with
these weak endeavours, the constancy of affection from the sincere
lover of your deserts in honour,

JOHN FORD.

1–2 *John ... Turvey* John Mordaunt (*c.* 1599–1642), a court favourite, created 1st Earl of Peter-
    borough in 1628

  8 *freedom* distinction

10–12 *Your ... presentment* Mordaunt had enjoyed seeing the play in performance ('in the
    action'), which led Ford to dedicate to him the printed version ('this presentment').

  14 *gravity ... lightness* playing on (*a*) seriousness versus levity and (*b*) physical heaviness
    versus lightness; 'the lightness of the title' also carries an implication of sexual licen-
    tiousness (with reference to its use of the word 'whore').

14–15 *otherwise ... guilt* Ford himself would not have approved the use of a licentious title in
    a less serious play.

The Persons of the Play ed. (Q's list of 'The Actors' Names' appears in the Appendix.) For details of the names' direct literary sources, see the Introduction, p.5.

ANNABELLA The dialogue indicates that her hair is blonde (II.v.52–3), which was considered exceptionally beautiful in the period.

GIOVANNI The name is pronounced with four syllables (rather than three as in modern Italian).

PUTANA From the sixteenth-century Italian word *puttana*, defined in *World* as 'a whore, a harlot, a strumpet, a quean'.

FRIAR BONAVENTURA Named after the philosopher and theologian, St Bonaventure (1221–74); he became head of the Franciscan order in 1257, in succession to John of Parma (*c.* 1209–57), and became a Cardinal in 1273. If the character is portrayed as a Franciscan like his namesake (and like most other friars in English Renaissance drama), then his habit will be grey; the other possibilities are black (Dominican) or white (Carmelite).

VASQUES His name 'indicates that he is the only Spaniard' (Lomax).

GRIMALDI Perhaps the name draws associations from the Italian word *grimaldelli*, defined in *World* as 'a kind of darting weapon'.

DONADO The dialogue indicates that he is bearded (II.iv.22).

POGGIO Named after the Florentine scholar and historian, Gian Francesco Poggio Bracciolini (1380–1459), who was the subject of a sardonic epigram (I. 20) by Jacopo Sannazaro.

HIPPOLITA Named after two characters in classical mythology: Hippolyta the Amazon queen conquered by Theseus, and Hippolyte, the lustful Queen of Iolcus who fell in love with Peleus and, when he refused to enter an adulterous relationship with her, avenged herself by accusing him of trying to seduce her.

PHILOTIS From the Greek word *philotes* (= love, affection). Ford had made extensive use of significant Greek names in *The Broken Heart*, probably written soon before *'Tis Pity She's a Whore*.

Parma A city in Lombardy, about 220 miles north of Rome. It had been an independent state since 1545 (see note to I.ii.77), and in Ford's time was known as a flourishing mercantile centre; compare *The Fatal Marriage* (1620s), 972–3: 'a richer treasure . . . / Than Parma's custom comes to by the year'.

THE PERSONS OF THE PLAY

ANNABELLA, *Florio's daughter*

GIOVANNI, *Annabella's brother*

SIGNOR FLORIO, *a citizen of Parma*

PUTANA, *Annabella's tutoress*

FRIAR BONAVENTURA, *Giovanni's tutor and confessor*

LORD SORANZO, *a nobleman, Annabella's suitor*

VASQUES, *Soranzo's Spanish servant*

GRIMALDI, *a Roman gentleman and soldier, Annabella's suitor*

SIGNOR DONADO, *a citizen of Parma*

BERGETTO, *Donado's nephew, Annabella's suitor*

POGGIO, *Bergetto's servant*

HIPPOLITA, *Soranzo's former paramour*

RICHARDETTO, *Hippolita's husband, believed dead; disguised as a physician*

PHILOTIS, *Richardetto's niece*

THE CARDINAL, *the Pope's Nuncio*

His Servant

Officers of the watch, Ladies, Banditti, Attendants

The action takes place in Parma

'Tis Pity She's a Whore

[Act I, Scene i]

Enter FRIAR *and* GIOVANNI

FRIAR
Dispute no more in this, for know, young man,
These are no school-points: nice philosophy
May tolerate unlikely arguments,
But Heaven admits no jest. Wits that presumed
On wit too much by striving how to prove   5
There was no God, with foolish grounds of art
Discovered first the nearest way to hell,
And filled the world with devilish atheism.
Such questions, youth, are fond, for better 'tis
To bless the sun, than reason why it shines;   10
Yet he thou talk'st of is above the sun.
No more! I may not hear it.
GIOVANNI   Gentle father,
To you I have unclasped my burdened soul,
Emptied the storehouse of my thoughts and heart,
Made myself poor of secrets, have not left   15
Another word untold which hath not spoke
All what I ever durst or think, or know;
And yet is here the comfort I shall have?
Must I not do what all men else may – love?

---

1   *young man* Giovanni's name literally implies youth in Italian.
2   *school-points* issues in a university disputation (used to train students in the practice of
    logical reasoning; see Introduction, p. xviii)
    nice over-precise
4   *Heaven* a periphrasis for God, here respectful, sometimes merely polite; the word is cap-
    italized when used in this sense
    admits tolerates
4–5 *Wits . . . much* Clever people whose intellect made them arrogantly presumptuous
6   *grounds of art* scholarly proofs
9   *fond* foolish, pointless
11 *he . . . of* God
17 *All what* Everything
    durst dared
    or . . . or either . . . or

FRIAR
   Yes, you may love, fair son.
GIOVANNI   Must I not praise   20
   That beauty which, if framed anew, the gods
   Would make a god of if they had it there,
   And kneel to it, as I do kneel to them?
FRIAR
   Why, foolish madman!
GIOVANNI   Shall a peevish sound,
   A customary form, from man to man,   25
   Of brother and of sister, be a bar
   'Twixt my perpetual happiness and me?
   Say that we had one father, say one womb
   (Curse to my joys!) gave both us life and birth:
   Are we not therefore each to other bound   30
   So much the more by nature, by the links
   Of blood, of reason (nay, if you will have't,
   Even of religion), to be ever one,
   One soul, one flesh, one love, one heart, one all?
FRIAR
   Have done, unhappy youth, for thou art lost.   35
GIOVANNI
   Shall then, for that I am her brother born,
   My joys be ever banished from her bed?
   No, father: in your eyes I see the change
   Of pity and compassion; from your age,
   As from a sacred oracle, distils   40
   The life of counsel. Tell me, holy man,
   What cure shall give me ease in these extremes?
FRIAR
   Repentance, son, and sorrow for this sin;
   For thou hast moved a majesty above

21–2 *the gods . . . there* Giovanni speaks in terms of the classical gods, who are neither
      omnipresent nor omniscient: they exist in a definite location ('there') and their appre-
      ciation of beauty is dependent on its physical presence. The wording accordingly
      establishes his distance from the Friar's Christian discourse.
24 *peevish* (*a*) meaningless; (*b*) spiteful
25 *A customary . . . man* terminology which carries only the authority of human custom
      (rather than divine law)
32 *blood* Giovanni means 'consanguinity', but the word also carries the relevant secondary
      meaning, 'lust'.
35 *unhappy* ill-fated

With thy unrangèd almost blasphemy.   45
GIOVANNI
  O, do not speak of that, dear confessor.
FRIAR
  Art thou, my son, that miracle of wit
  Who once, within these three months, wert esteemed
  A wonder of thine age, throughout Bologna?
  How did the university applaud   50
  Thy government, behaviour, learning, speech,
  Sweetness, and all that could make up a man!
  I was proud of my tutelage, and chose
  Rather to leave my books than part with thee:
  I did so – but the fruits of all my hopes   55
  Are lost in thee, as thou art in thyself.
  O Giovanni! Hast thou left the schools
  Of knowledge, to converse with lust and death?
  For death waits on thy lust. Look through the world,
  And thou shalt see a thousand faces shine   60
  More glorious than this idol thou ador'st:
  Leave her, and take thy choice;'tis much less sin,
  Though in such games as those they lose that win.
GIOVANNI
  It were more ease to stop the ocean
  From floats and ebbs, than to dissuade my vows.   65
FRIAR
  Then I have done, and in thy wilful flames

45 *unrangèd* limitless
    almost It is ambiguous whether the word is being used to qualify 'unrangèd' or 'blas-
    phemy'.
49 *A wonder . . . age* i.e. a precociously brilliant student
    Bologna ed. (*Bononia* Q); a city in the Papal States, about 50 miles from Parma, where
    the play is set; it was the seat of Italy's oldest university, founded in the twelfth century.
    The university owed its association with free-thinking, relevant to Giovanni, in part to
    the philosopher Pietro Pomponazzi (1462–1525), who there wrote his treatise (published
    1516) denying the immortality of the soul.
51 *government* self-discipline
58 *death* spiritual death
60–1 *shine . . . glorious* appear more beautiful
62–3 *'tis . . . win* The Friar's proposal is a compromise: because he is committed to celibacy
    (as both academic and friar), any sexual relationship is in his eyes a loser's game, but
    most are less sinful than the incest Giovanni desires.
65 *floats and ebbs* high and low tides
    vows wishes, promises
66 *wilful flames* self-willed heat (of sexuality)

[49]

Already see thy ruin: Heaven is just.
Yet hear my counsel.

GIOVANNI   As a voice of life.

FRIAR

Hie to thy father's house, there lock thee fast
Alone within thy chamber, then fall down   70
On both thy knees, and grovel on the ground.
Cry to thy heart, wash every word thou utter'st
In tears, and, if't be possible, of blood.
Beg Heaven to cleanse the leprosy of lust
That rots thy soul. Acknowledge what thou art,   75
A wretch, a worm, a nothing. Weep, sigh, pray
Three times a day, and three times every night.
For seven days' space do this; then if thou find'st
No change in thy desires, return to me:
I'll think on remedy. Pray for thyself   80
At home, whilst I pray for thee here. Away,
My blessing with thee. We have need to pray.

GIOVANNI

All this I'll do, to free me from the rod
Of vengeance; else I'll swear my fate's my God.   *Exeunt*

[Act I, Scene ii]

Enter GRIMALDI *and* VASQUES *ready to fight*

VASQUES

Come sir, stand to your tackling. If you prove craven I'll make you
run quickly.

---

69 *Hie* Go speedily
73 *tears . . . of blood* tears expressing the most absolute penitence
74 *leprosy* a disfiguring disease which eats away the skin, leaving red lesions; it was often
    used as a metaphor for moral or sexual corruption

 0 s.d. *ready to fight* The phrase probably refers only to Vasques: both men are armed, but
    the ensuing dialogue indicates that Grimaldi is initially unwilling to fight, so only Vasques'
    sword is drawn.
 1 *stand . . . tackling* stand and fight (tackling = weapons); a variant of the military com-
    mand 'stand to arms'(= prepare for combat)
1–2 prose ed. (Come . . . *Crauen,* / I'le . . . quickly Q)

GRIMALDI

Thou art no equal match for me.

VASQUES

Indeed I never went to the wars to bring home news, nor cannot
play the mountebank for a meal's meat, and swear I got my wounds   5
in the field. See you these grey hairs? They'll not flinch for a bloody
nose! Wilt thou to this gear?

GRIMALDI

Why, slave, think'st thou I'll balance my reputation with a
cast-suit? Call thy master, he shall know that I dare –

VASQUES

Scold like a cotquean, that's your profession, thou poor   10
shadow of a soldier. I will make thee know my master keeps
servants thy betters in quality and performance. Comest thou to
fight, or prate?

GRIMALDI

Neither with thee. I am a Roman and a gentleman, one that have
got mine honour with expense of blood.   15

VASQUES

You are a lying coward and a fool. Fight, or by these hilts I'll kill
thee.   [GRIMALDI *draws his sword*]

3   *no equal* Grimaldi is a gentleman, Vasques a servant; the inequality is underlined by Grimaldi's
    use of the familiar 'thou' pronoun (whereas Vasques at first uses the more respectful 'you').

4–6   *I never . . . field* Vasques goads Grimaldi with an accusation of cowardice and mendac-
    ity. Mountebanks (itinerant medicine pedlars) were notorious for telling exaggerated
    lies about their wares, and Vasques suggests that Grimaldi's claims of military honour
    are in the same category: that he was never at the wars as a combatant, only a reporter,
    and has lied about his wounds to make himself a welcome guest at Florio's table. (The
    scene apparently takes place during an all-male dinner – here a mid-day meal – for the
    three suitors; see also lines 103–4 below.)

7   *gear* the matter in hand (i.e. the fight between them)

8   *balance* equate

9   *cast-suit* a base person who wears cast-off clothes

10   *cotquean* low-born housewife
    your profession the category of person in which you belong

11   *shadow* unreal image

12   *servants thy betters* servants who are thy betters

14–15   prose ed. (Neither . . . thee, / I . . . got / Mine . . . blood Q)

15   *expense of blood* shedding of his own blood

16   *by these hilts* An asseveration, but also referring to Grimaldi's undrawn sword, with its
    hilt pointing forward; the plural, *hilts*, may suggest that he is armed with rapier and dag-
    ger, the latter used for parrying (though compare II.vi.73 and note).

Brave, my lord! You'll fight.

GRIMALDI

Provoke me not, for if thou dost –

VASQUES

Have at you!   *They fight;* GRIMALDI *hath the worst*   20

Enter FLORIO, DONADO, SORANZO

FLORIO

What mean these sudden broils so near my doors?
Have you not other places but my house
To vent the spleen of your disordered bloods?
Must I be haunted still with such unrest
As not to eat or sleep in peace at home?   25
Is this your love, Grimaldi? Fie, 'tis naught.

DONADO

And, Vasques, I may tell thee 'tis not well
To broach these quarrels. You are ever forward
In seconding contentions.

Enter above ANNABELLA *and* PUTANA

FLORIO   What's the ground?

SORANZO

That, with your patience, signors, I'll resolve: 30
This gentleman, whom fame reports a soldior
(For else I know not) rivals me in love
To Signor Florio's daughter, to whose ears
He still prefers his suit, to my disgrace,
Thinking the way to recommend himself   35
Is to disparage me in his report.

18 *Brave . . . lord* If 'Brave' is an adjective (as punctuated here), the line is a sarcastic taunt;
    if it is a verb, however, the sense is 'How dare you challenge my lord!'
21 *sudden* rash, violent
23 *spleen* a fit of anger or proud temper
26 *naught* worthless
29 *seconding* stirring up
    the ground the cause of the argument
29 s.d. *above* on the stage balcony
30 *resolve* explain, clarify
32 *else* otherwise. Soranzo says, provocatively that Grimaldi's reputation ('fame') is the only
    soldierly thing about him
34 *prefers* advances

But know, Grimaldi, though maybe thou art
My equal in thy blood, yet this bewrays
A lowness in thy mind, which, wert thou noble,
Thou wouldst as much disdain as I do thee   40
For this unworthiness. [*To* FLORIO] And on this ground
I willed my servant to correct this tongue,
Holding a man so base no match for me.

VASQUES
And had not your sudden coming prevented us, I had let my
gentleman blood under the gills. [*To* GRIMALDI] I should   45
have wormed you, sir, for running mad.

GRIMALDI
I'll be revenged, Soranzo.

VASQUES
On a dish of warm broth to stay your stomach – do, honest
innocence, do! Spoon-meat is a wholesomer diet than a Spanish
blade.   50

GRIMALDI
Remember this.

SORANZO   I fear thee not, Grimaldi.

                                              Exit GRIMALDI

FLORIO
My lord Soranzo, this is strange to me,
Why you should storm, having my word engaged:
Owing her heart, what need you doubt her ear?

38   *bewrays* reveals, exposes (implying that the thing revealed is shameful)
42   *this* Q; other editors, assuming that Soranzo is still speaking to Grimaldi, have emended
     to 'thy'. The recurrence of the word 'ground', however, suggests to me that he is address-
     ing Florio in conclusion to his answer to the question Florio asked in line 29, 'What's the
     ground?' The Q reading's unusual wording (as distinct from, say, 'his') conveys his dis-
     dainful contempt for his rival.
44   *had not* ed. (had Q)
44–5 *let . . . gills* The metaphor is of a Renaissance doctor drawing off infected blood to cure
     the patient. A man's gills are the fleshy area under his jaw: Vasques is saying he would
     have cut Grimaldi's throat. The phrase may also suggest that Grimaldi has become red-
     faced with anger or exertion.
46   *wormed . . . mad* To worm a dog was to cut its lytta, a ligament under its tongue, as a pre-
     ventative against rabies ('running mad'); Grimaldi has also 'run mad' with anger.
48   *stay your stomach* (*a*) satisfy your appetite; (*b*) check your aggression
49   *Spoon-meat* Liquid food typically eaten by invalids and toothless people
49–50 *a Spanish blade* Vasques' sword
53   *engaged* pledged
54   *Owing* Possessing.

Losers may talk by law of any game.   55

VASQUES

Yet the villainy of words, Signor Florio, may be such as
would make any unspleened dove choleric. Blame not my
lord in this.

FLORIO

Be you more silent.

I would not for my wealth my daughter's love   60
Should cause the spilling of one drop of blood.
Vasques, put up. Let's end this fray in wine.

       Exeunt [FLORIO, DONADO, SORANZO *and* VASQUES]

PUTANA

How like you this, child? Here's threatening, challenging, quar-
relling, and fighting, on every side, and all is for your sake. You
had need look to yourself, charge, you'll be stolen away sleeping   65
else shortly.

ANNABELLA

But tut'ress, such a life gives no content
To me: my thoughts are fixed on other ends.
Would you would leave me.

PUTANA

Leave you? No marvel else! Leave me no leaving, charge,   70
this is love outright. Indeed, I blame you not, you have choice fit
for the best lady in Italy.

ANNABELLA

Pray do not talk so much.

PUTANA

Take the worst with the best – there's Grimaldi the soldier, a very

---

  55 The winner of a game should magnanimously allow the losers to express their disap-
pointment or resentment; proverbial (Tilley, L. 458).

  56 *villainy* ed. (villaine Q)

  57 *make . . . choleric* In contemporary psychology, choler was the 'humour' (bodily fluid)
which caused anger when an excessive amount was present in the blood-stream. It was
believed that doves' livers did not secrete gall (thought to be a form of choler); thus to
make a dove choleric is to enrage even the mildest of creatures.

56–8 prose ed. (Yet . . . such, /As . . . Chollerick, / Blame . . . this Q)

  62 *put up* sheathe your sword

  68 *ends* matters

  70 *No marvel else!* No wonder [you want me to do so]! Putana assumes that Annabella
wishes to be left alone for sexual reasons.

70–2 prose ed. (Leaue . . . (Chardge) / This . . . haue / Choyce . . . *Italy* Q)

well-timbered fellow: they say he is a Roman, nephew to   75
the Duke Monferrato; they say he did good service in
the wars against the Milanese. But faith, charge, I do not like him,
an't be for nothing but for being a soldier: one amongst twenty
of your skirmishing captains but have some privy maim or
other that mars their standing upright. I like him the   80
worse. He crinkles so much in the hams – though he might
serve if there were no more men. Yet he's not the man
I would choose.

ANNABELLA
Fie, how thou pratest.

PUTANA
As I am a very woman, I like Signor Soranzo well: he is   85
wise; and what is more, rich; and what is more than that,
kind; and what is more than all this, a nobleman. Such a one,
were I the fair Annabella myself, I would wish and pray
for. Then he is bountiful; besides he is handsome; and,
by my troth, I think wholesome – and that's news in a gallant   90
of three-and-twenty. Liberal, that I know; loving, that
you know; and a man sure, else he could never ha'

---

75 *well-timbered* well built. (The metaphor is of a house.)
76 *Duke Monferrato* ed. (Duke *Mount Ferratto* Q). Monferrato was a small, strategically
    important state in north-west Italy, which was annexed to the state of Mantua in 1536,
    and became a duchy in 1574.
77 *the wars . . . Milanese* Parma was part of the Duchy of Milan until annexed to the
    Papal States in 1512; it was later incorporated into the Duchy of Piacenza and Parma in
    1545. Milan still pressed its claim to Parma, and recaptured Piacenza in 1547; war fol-
    lowed in 1551–2.
    Milanese ed. (*Millanoys* Q)
77 *an't* if it
78 *one . . . twenty . . . but have* there is not one amongst twenty . . . who do not have
79 *privy maim* hidden wound
80 *mars . . . upright* makes them impotent (playing on the usual meaning of 'standing
    upright'; but, since the wound is 'privy', the sexual sense is dominant)
81 *crinkles . . . in the hams* (*a*) bows obsequiously; (*b*) shrinks from his (sexual) purpose
85 *very* true
    Signor Soranzo Putana (ignorantly?) 'demotes' Soranzo, who is everywhere else addressed
    as 'Lord Soranzo', to 'Signor' (a polite term of address, similar to the modern English
    'Mister').
90 *wholesome* uninfected by venereal disease
91 *Liberal* Generous, especially with money; that Putana says she knows this implies that
    he has bribed her to promote his suit (compare II.vi.14–20, where she cadges money
    from Donado for similar alleged services).
92 *a man* i.e. not impotent

purchased such a good name with Hippolita the lusty
widow in her husband's lifetime. An 'twere but for that report,
sweetheart, would a were thine! Commend a man for his   95
qualities, but take a husband as he is a plain-sufficient, naked man:
such a one is for your bed, and such a one is Signor Soranzo,
my life for't.

ANNABELLA

Sure the woman took her morning's draught too soon.

Enter BERGETTO *and* POGGIO

PUTANA

But look, sweetheart, look what thing comes now: here's another   100
of your ciphers to fill up the number. O, brave old ape in a silken
coat! Observe.

BERGETTO

Didst thou think, Poggio, that I would spoil my new clothes, and
leave my dinner to fight?

POGGIO

No sir, I did not take you for so arrant a baby.   105

BERGETTO

I am wiser than so; for I hope, Poggio, thou never heard'st of an
elder brother that was a coxcomb, didst, Poggio?

POGGIO

Never indeed sir, as long as they had either land or money left them
to inherit.

---

93   *good name* high regard
95   *would a were* 'a' is the unstressed form of 'he'
96   *qualities* skills, accomplishments
99   *took . . . soon* started drinking alcohol too early in the day; a 'morning's draught' was lit-
      erally a drink of wine or beer taken in the morning, often before work, so Annabella is
      probably speaking jocularly rather than with irritation (especially if the scene takes place
      around mid-day, as it seems to).
99   s.d. Bergetto and Poggio enter on the main stage, with Annabella and Putana looking
      down on them from above.
100–2 prose ed. (But . . . now: / Here's . . . number: / Oh . . . obserue Q)
  101   *ciphers* nonentities
         brave finely clad
101–2 *ape . . . coat* i.e. a fool dressed in finery
103–4 prose ed. (Did'st . . . my / New . . . fight Q)
  104   *leave my dinner* All Florio's other guests broke off their meal because of the fight
         between Grimaldi and Vasques; Bergetto has stayed behind to finish his.
106–7 prose ed. (I . . . thou / Neuer . . . Coxcomb, / Did'st *Poggio*? Q)
  107   *elder brother* Implying an heir (with reference to himself as Donado's heir).
         coxcomb fool

BERGETTO

Is it possible, Poggio? O monstrous! Why, I'll undertake,   110
with a handful of silver, to buy a headful of wit at any time.
But, sirrah, I have another purchase in hand: I shall have
the wench, mine uncle says. I will but wash my face, and
shift socks, and then have at her i'faith! – Mark my pace,
Poggio.   [*He walks affectedly*]   115

POGGIO

Sir, I have seen an ass and a mule trot the Spanish pavan with a
better grace, I know not how often.

Exeunt [BERGETTO *and* POGGIO]

ANNABELLA

This idiot haunts me too.

PUTANA

Ay, ay, he needs no description. The rich magnifico that is
below with your father, charge, Signor Donado, his uncle,   120
for that he means to make this his cousin a golden calf, thinks
that you will be a right Israelite and fall down to him
presently; but I hope I have tutored you better. They say a
fool's bauble is a lady's playfellow; yet you having wealth enough,
you need not cast upon the dearth of flesh at any rate: hang him,   125
innocent!

Enter GIOVANNI

ANNABELLA

But see, Putana, see; what blessed shape
Of some celestial creature now appears?
What man is he, that with such sad aspect

114 *shift* change
      Mark my pace Watch how I walk
116 *the Spanish pavan* a slow, stately dance
119 *magnifico* wealthy man
121 *golden calf* Alluding to the idol worshipped by the Israelites in the wilderness
      (Exodus 32); Donado is said to expect that Bergetto's riches will make Annabella 'fall
      down to' him (meaning both worship him and accept him as a sexual partner in mar-
      riage), even though he is a 'mooncalf' (= a simpleton).
123 *presently* immediately
123–4 *a fool's . . . playfellow* Proverbial (Tilley, F. 528); 'bauble' means both a professional fool's
      stick with a carved head, and a penis.
125 *cast . . . flesh* take decisions (literally, calculate) based on a shortage of male suitors
      (literally, penises); implying that she need not consider taking someone like Bergetto as
      her husband.

Walks careless of himself?

PUTANA   Where?

ANNABELLA   Look below.   130

PUTANA

O, 'tis your brother, sweet –

ANNABELLA   Ha!

PUTANA   'Tis your brother.

ANNABELLA

  Sure 'tis not he: this is some woeful thing
  Wrapped up in grief, some shadow of a man.
  Alas, he beats his breast, and wipes his eyes
  Drowned all in tears; methinks I hear him sigh.   135
  Let's down, Putana, and partake the cause;
  I know my brother, in the love he bears me,
  Will not deny me partage in his sadness.
  My soul is full of heaviness and fear.

                    Exeunt [from above ANNABELLA *and* PUTANA]

GIOVANNI

  Lost, I am lost: my fates have doomed my death.   140
  The more I strive, I love; the more I love,
  The less I hope. I see my ruin, certain.
  What judgement or endeavours could apply
  To my incurable and restless wounds
  I throughly have examined, but in vain.   145
  O that it were not in religion sin
  To make our love a god, and worship it!
  I have even wearied Heaven with prayers, dried up
  The spring of my continual tears, even starved
  My veins with daily fasts: what wit or art   150
  Could counsel, I have practised. But alas,
  I find all these but dreams, and old men's tales
  To fright unsteady youth: I'm still the same.
  Or I must speak, or burst. 'Tis not, I know,
  My lust, but 'tis my fate that leads me on.   155
  Keep fear and low, faint-hearted shame with slaves!

---

136 *partake* be told (and so share)
138 *partage* a share
145 *throughly* thoroughly
150 *wit* intellect
156 *Keep fear and . . . shame* May fear and . . . shame dwell

I'll tell her that I love her, though my heart
Were rated at the price of that attempt.

Enter ANNABELLA *and* PUTANA

O me! She comes.
ANNABELLA   Brother.
GIOVANNI   [*Aside*] If such a thing
  As courage dwell in men, ye heavenly powers,   160
  Now double all that virtue in my tongue.
ANNABELLA
  Why brother, will you not speak to me?
GIOVANNI
  Yes; how d'ee, sister?
ANNABELLA
  Howsoever I am, methinks you are not well.
PUTANA
  Bless us, why are you so sad, sir?   165
GIOVANNI
  Let me entreat you leave us awhile, Putana.
  Sister, I would be private with you.
ANNABELLA
  Withdraw, Putana.
PUTANA
  I will. [*Aside*] If this were any other company for her, I should
  think my absence an office of some credit; but I will leave them   170
  together.   *Exit*
GIOVANNI
  Come sister, lend your hand, let's walk together.
  I hope you need not blush to walk with me;
  Here's none but you and I.
ANNABELLA   How's this?
GIOVANNI
  Faith, I mean no harm.   175

157–8 *though . . . attempt* though attempting it should cost me my heart
  158 *rated* valued
  158 s.d. ed. (after line 159a in Q)
  163 *d'ee* do you (a contraction often used by Ford)
  169 *I will* printed on a separate line in Q
  170 *an office . . . credit* a favour deserving reward (with the ironic secondary meaning, 'post
     of honour')
  173 Annabella would have cause to blush with sexual modesty if walking alone with any man
     but her brother.

ANNABELLA
> Harm?

GIOVANNI
> No, good faith; how is't with 'ee?

ANNABELLA
> [*Aside*] I trust he be not frantic. [*To him*] I am very well,
> brother.

GIOVANNI
> Trust me, but I am sick; I fear so sick   180
> 'Twill cost my life.

ANNABELLA
> Mercy forbid it! 'Tis not so, I hope.

GIOVANNI
> I think you love me, sister.

ANNABELLA
> Yes, you know I do.

GIOVANNI
> I know't, indeed. – You're very fair.   185

ANNABELLA
> Nay then, I see you have a merry sickness.

GIOVANNI
> That's as it proves. The poets feign, I read,
> That Juno for her forehead did exceed
> All other goddesses; but I durst swear
> Your forehead exceeds hers, as hers did theirs.   190

ANNABELLA
> Troth, this is pretty!

GIOVANNI   Such a pair of stars
> As are thine eyes would, like Promethean fire,
> If gently glanced, give life to senseless stones.

---

178 *frantic* deranged
178–9 prose ed. (I . . . franticke— / I . . . brother Q)
  185 *You're* ed. (y'are Q)
        fair beautiful
  187 *The poets* ed. (they Poets Q)
  188 *Juno* the classical goddess of marriage, twin sister and wife of Jupiter
  192 *Promethean fire* a life-giving force; in classical mythology, Prometheus stole fire from heaven
        and, in some versions of the story, used it to animate the first human beings. Ford may be
        recalling Shakespeare's usage in *Love's Labours Lost* (IV.iii.327), where Promethean fire is also
        an attribute of beautiful women's eyes. The whole passage plays on the two principal mean-
        ings of 'glance', to look swiftly and to strike obliquely (here against a stone, producing sparks).

ANNABELLA
  Fie upon 'ee!
GIOVANNI
  The lily and the rose, most sweetly strange,   195
  Upon your dimpled cheeks do strive for change.
  Such lips would tempt a saint; such hands as those
  Would make an anchorite lascivious.
ANNABELLA
  D'ee mock me, or flatter me?
GIOVANNI
  If you would see a beauty more exact   200
  Than art can counterfeit or nature frame,
  Look in your glass, and there behold your own.
ANNABELLA
  O, you arc a trim youth.
GIOVANNI
  Here.   *Offers his dagger to her*
ANNABELLA What to do?
GIOVANNI   And here's my breast: strike home.
  Rip up my bosom: there thou shalt behold   205
  A heart in which is writ the truth I speak.
  Why stand 'ee?
ANNABELLA   Are you earnest?
GIOVANNI   Yes, most earnest.
  You cannot love?
ANNABELLA   Whom?
GIOVANNI   Me. My tortured soul
  Hath felt affliction in the heat of death.
  O, Annabella, I am quite undone: 210
  The love of thee, my sister, and the view
  Of thy immortal beauty hath untuned
  All harmony both of my rest and life.
  Why d'ee not strike?

195 *strange* in opposition (to one another)
196 *change* interchange; Annabella is blushing and blanching by turns.
198 *anchorite* a hermit or religious recluse; a byword for the absence of sexual desire
202 *glass* mirror
203 *trim* handsome
207 *stand* hesitate
209 *affliction . . . death* suffering so intense that it resembles or threatens death

ANNABELLA   Forbid it, my just fears.
If this be true, 'twere fitter I were dead.   215
GIOVANNI
Two, Annabella? 'Tis no time to jest.
I have too long suppressed the hidden flames
That almost have consumed me. I have spent
Many a silent night in sighs and groans,
Ran over all my thoughts, despised my fate,   220
Reasoned against the reasons of my love,
Done all that smoothed-cheek Virtue could advise,
But found all bootless: 'tis my destiny
That you must either love, or I must die.
ANNABELLA
Comes this in sadness from you?
GIOVANNI   Let some mischief   225
Befall me soon, if I dissemble aught.
ANNABELLA
You are my brother, Giovanni.
GIOVANNI   You
My sister, Annabella. I know this,
And could afford you instance why to love
So much the more for this, to which intent   230
Wise Nature first in your creation meant
To make you mine; else't had been sin and foul
To share one beauty to a double soul.
Nearness in birth or blood doth but persuade
A nearer nearness in affection.   235
I have asked counsel of the holy Church,
Who tells me I may love you; and 'tis just
That, since I may, I should; and will, yes will.
Must I now live, or die?
ANNABELLA   Live. Thou hast won
The field, and never fought: what thou hast urged,   240

220 *despised* attempted to defy
222 *smoothed-cheek* clean-shaven (implying either youth and inexperience or slippery
      persuasiveness); the term may also be a misprint for 'smooth-cheeked'.
223 *bootless* useless, ineffectual
225 *in sadness* sincerely, earnestly
226 *aught* anything, in any respect
228–33 Giovanni offers her an argument ('afford ... instance') in favour of incest: having already
      established that they are physically alike in beauty, he argues that they must also have a
      corresponding affinity of souls which, in neoplatonic philosophy, was the origin of love.

[62]

My captive heart had long ago resolved.
I blush to tell thee (but I'll tell thee now),
For every sigh that thou hast spent for me,
I have sighed ten; for every tear shed twenty;
And not so much for that I loved, as that   245
I durst not say I loved, nor scarcely think it.

GIOVANNI
   Let not this music be a dream, ye gods,
   For pity's sake I beg 'ee!   *She kneels*

ANNABELLA   On my knees,
   Brother, even by our mother's dust, I charge you,
   Do not betray me to your mirth or hate: 250
   Love me, or kill me, brother.   *He kneels*

GIOVANNI   On my knees,
   Sister, even by my mother's dust I charge you,
   Do not betray me to your mirth or hate:
   Love me, or kill me, sister.

ANNABELLA
   You mean good sooth then?

GIOVANNI   In good troth I do,   255
   And so do you, I hope. Say: I'm in earnest.

ANNABELLA
   I'll swear't, and I.

GIOVANNI   And I, and by this kiss –   *Kisses her*
   Once more. [*Kisses her*] Yet once more. [*Kisses her*] Now let's rise,
      by this.   [*They rise*]
   I would not change this minute for Elysium.
   What must we now do?

ANNABELLA   What you will.

GIOVANNI   Come then: 260
   After so many tears as we have wept,
   Let's learn to court in smiles, to kiss and sleep.   *Exeunt*

---

255 *good sooth* truthfully
259 *change* exchange
     Elysium in classical mythology, the posthumous destination of the virtuous; the pagan
     equivalent of heaven
260 *What you will* Whatever you like (with a sexual implication)

[Act I, Scene iii]

Enter FLORIO *and* DONADO

FLORIO

Signor Donado, you have said enough,
I understand you, but would have you know
I will not force my daughter 'gainst her will.
You see I have but two, a son and her;
And he is so devoted to his book,   5
As, I must tell you true, I doubt his health.
Should he miscarry, all my hopes rely
Upon my girl. As for worldly fortune,
I am, I thank my stars, blessed with enough.
My care is how to match her to her liking: 10
I would not have her marry wealth, but love;
And if she like your nephew, let him have her.
Here's all that I can say.

DONADO   Sir, you say well,
Like a true father, and for my part, I,
If the young folks can like ('twixt you and me),   15
Will promise to assure my nephew presently
Three thousand florins yearly during life,
And, after I am dead, my whole estate.

FLORIO

'Tis a fair proffer, sir. Meantime your nephew
Shall have free passage to commence his suit.   20
If he can thrive, he shall have my consent.
So for this time I'll leave you, signor.   *Exit*

DONADO   Well,
Here's hope yet, if my nephew would have wit;
But he is such another dunce, I fear
He'll never win the wench. When I was young   25

---

7   *miscarry* die prematurely, without continuing the family line
16 *presently* now
17 *Three thousand florins* Roughly equivalent to £250; a substantial but not lavish
    annual income for a landed gentleman.
20 *free passage* access to speak to Annabella

[64]

I could have done't, i' faith, and so shall he
If he will learn of me.

Enter BERGETTO *and* POGGIO

And in good time
He comes himself.

POGGIO

How now, Bergetto, whither away so fast?

BERGETTO

O uncle, I have heard the strangest news that ever came out of the   30
mint – have I not, Poggio?

POGGIO

Yes indeed, sir.

DONADO

What news, Bergetto?

BERGETTO

Why, look ye uncle, my barber told me just now that there
is a fellow come to town, who undertakes to make a mill go   35
without the mortal help of any water or wind, only with sandbags!
And this fellow hath a strange horse, a most excellent beast
I'll assure you, uncle, my barber says, whose head, to the wonder
of all Christian people, stands just behind where his tail is. Is't
not true, Poggio?   40

---

27   s.d. ed.; after line 28 in Q

27   *in good time* at the appropriate moment, 'as if on cue'

29   s.p. *POGGIO* Q. The implied stage action has Bergetto rushing across the stage, a man
with his mind on the fairground and anxious to get there quickly, while Poggio fol-
lows calling after: he may just be struggling to keep up (the verb *to podge*, which is
echoed in his name, means to dawdle), or he may be giving Bergetto a gentle hint not
to rush rudely past his uncle. All other editors since Weber reassign the line to Donado, primarily because it is uncharacteristic for Poggio to address his master by name;
but this makes good enough sense either as a lapse of courtesy in the haste of the
moment or a calculated way of getting Bergetto's attention and so forestalling the *faux
pas* he is about to commit.

30–1   *news . . . mint* the newest news. The reference to the mint is double-edged: Bergetto means
it to suggest the news's authenticity (in that the mint is the source of the currency), but
minting is also a process of fabrication.

34   *uncle*, ed. (uncle? Q)

35–6   *to make . . . sandbags* This probably refers to a perpetual motion machine.

37–39   *a strange horse . . . tail is* A famous fairground fraud: punters were charged to see this
wondrous animal, which turned out to be an ordinary horse with its tail tied to a manger
(where its head would normally be).

POGGIO

So the barber swore, forsooth.

DONADO

And you are running thither?

BERGETTO

Ay, forsooth, uncle.

DONADO

Wilt thou be a fool still? Come, sir, you shall not go. You have more
mind of a puppet-play than on the business I told ye. Why, thou   45
great baby, wilt never have wit, wilt make thyself a May-game to
all the world?

POGGIO

Answer for yourself, master.

BERGETTO

Why, uncle, should I sit at home still, and not go abroad to see
fashions like other gallants?   50

DONADO

To see hobby-horses! What wise talk, I pray, had you with
Annabella, when you were at Signor Florio's house?

BERGETTO

O, the wench: Uds sa' me, uncle, I tickled her with a rare speech,
that I made her almost burst her belly with laughing.

DONADO

Nay, I think so; and what speech was't?   55

BERGETTO

What did I say, Poggio?

POGGIO

Forsooth, my master said that he loved her almost as well as he

---

41   *barber* Barbers were notorious purveyors of false news, so the line can be played with
     sardonic irony, introducing the possibility that Poggio is somewhat brighter than Bergetto.
     forsooth truly
42   *thither* ed. (hither Q)
45   *puppet-play* another traditional fairground entertainment
46   *wilt . . . wilt* ed. (wu't . . . wu't Q)
46   *May-game* laughing-stock
49   *still* constantly
     abroad out of doors
51   *hobby-horses* trivial pastimes; but the word also meant 'prostitutes', so Donado may alter-
     natively suspect that Bergetto has ulterior motives for going out, which would compromise
     his suit to Annabella
53   *Uds sa' me* an oath, minced from 'God save me'

loved parmesan, and swore – I'll be sworn for him – that she
wanted but such a nose as his was, to be as pretty a young woman
as any was in Parma.   60

DONADO
O gross!

BERGETTO
Nay uncle, then she asked me whether my father had any more
children than myself; and I said, 'No, 'twere better he should have
had his brains knocked out first.'

DONADO
This is intolerable.   65

BERGETTO
Then said she, 'Will Signor Donado your uncle leave you all his
wealth?'

DONADO
Ha! That was good, did she harp upon that string?

BERGETTO
Did she harp upon that string? Ay, that she did. I answered,
'Leave me all his wealth? Why, woman, he hath no other wit;   70
if he had, he should hear on't to his everlasting glory and confu-
sion. I know,' quoth I, 'I am his white boy, and will not be gulled.'
And with that she fell into a great smile, and went away. Nay,
I did fit her.

DONADO
Ah, sirrah, then I see there is no changing of nature. Well, Bergetto,   75
I fear thou wilt be a very ass still.

BERGETTO
I should be sorry for that, uncle.

DONADO
Come, come you home with me. Since you are no better a speaker,
I'll have you write to her after some courtly manner, and

---

58 *parmesan* (Q Parmasent). Probably an Italian style of drinking (*OED* B.2) rather than
    an absurd reference to parmesan cheese (though the latter tends to raise a bigger laugh
    in the modern theatre).
71 *glory* He means 'shame'; this kind of ignorant misapplication of words had been a com-
    mon source of comedy in drama since Shakespeare's time.
72 *white boy* a term of endearment for a favourite child
72 *gulled* duped, conned (i.e. deprived of his inheritance by fraud)
74 *fit her* answer her aptly
75–76 prose ed. (Ah . . . nature, / Well . . . still Q)

enclose some rich jewel in the letter.   80
BERGETTO
Ay marry, that will be excellent.
DONADO
Peace, innocent!
Once in my time I'll set my wits to school;
If all fail, 'tis but the fortune of a fool.
BERGETTO
Poggio, 'twill do, Poggio!   *Exeunt*   85

Act II [Scene i]

Enter GIOVANNI *and* ANNABELLA, *as from their
chamber*

GIOVANNI
Come, Annabella, no more sister now
But love, a name more gracious. Do not blush,
Beauty's sweet wonder, but be proud to know
That yielding thou hast conquered, and inflamed
A heart whose tribute is thy brother's life.   5
ANNABELLA
And mine is his. O, how these stol'n contents
Would print a modest crimson on my cheeks,
Had any but my heart's delight prevailed!
GIOVANNI
I marvel why the chaster of your sex
Should think this pretty toy called maidenhead   10

---

80   *enclose . . . letter* Envelopes were not used in the seventeenth century: the paper of
     the letter itself will be folded around the jewel to make a small packet, and then sealed
     with wax.

 0   s.d. *as from* This wording in seventeenth-century stage directions usually indicates some
     significant action by the characters; see Alan C. Dessen, *Elizabethan Stage Conventions
     and Modern Interpreters* (Cambridge, 1984), pp. 31–3. In this case, Giovanni and Annabella
     might be rearranging their clothes to suggest that they have come 'from their chamber'
     (= bedroom; i.e. from 'chambering' = sex).
 4   *yielding* giving up her virginity
 6   *contents* pleasures
10   *toy* a trivial thing
     maidenhead virginity (literally, a woman's hymen, pierced in her first sexual encounter)

So strange a loss, when, being lost, 'tis nothing,
And you are still the same.
ANNABELLA   'Tis well for you;
Now you can talk.
GIOVANNI   Music as well consists
In th'ear, as in the playing.
ANNABELLA   O, you're wanton!
Tell on't, you're best, do.
GIOVANNI   Thou wilt chide me, then.   15
Kiss me. [*They kiss*] So. Thus hung Jove on Leda's neck
And sucked divine ambrosia from her lips.
I envy not the mightiest man alive,
But hold myself, in being king of thee,
More great than were I king of all the world.   20
But I shall lose you, sweetheart.
ANNABELLA   But you shall not.
GIOVANNI
You must be married, mistress.
ANNABELLA   Yes, to whom?
GIOVANNI
Someone must have you.
ANNABELLA   You must.
GIOVANNI   Nay, some other.
ANNABELLA
Now prithee do not speak so without jesting:
You'll make me weep in earnest.
GIOVANNI   What, you will not!   25
But tell me, sweet, canst thou be dared to swear
That thou wilt live to me, and to no other?
ANNABELLA
By both our loves I dare; for didst thou know,

11 *nothing* (*a*) an insignificant thing; (*b*) a vagina
13–14 *Music . . . playing* Implying that you don't have to experience something directly to under-
         stand it (with reference to Giovanni's inability to share Annabella's female experience of
         losing her virginity).
16 *Thus . . . Leda's neck* In classical mythology, the god Jupiter (also known as Jove) visited
         the woman Leda in the shape of a swan, and fathered twins on her.
17 *ambrosia* the food of the classical gods; hence a byword for anything with a superlatively
         pleasant taste
25 *weep in earnest* truly cry; possibly she has feigned tears during the preceding jocular ban-
         ter
27 *live to me* live faithful to me

My Giovanni, how all suitors seem
To my eyes hateful, thou wouldst trust me then.   30
GIOVANNI
Enough, I take thy word. Sweet, we must part.
Remember what thou vowst: keep well my heart.
ANNABELLA
Will you be gone?
GIOVANNI   I must.
ANNABELLA
When to return?
GIOVANNI   Soon.
ANNABELLA   Look you do.
GIOVANNI   Farewell.   *Exit*
ANNABELLA
Go where thou wilt, in mind I'll keep thee here,   35
And where thou art, I know I shall be there.
Guardian!

Enter PUTANA

PUTANA
Child, how is't, child? Well, thank Heaven, ha?
ANNABELLA
O guardian, what a paradise of joy
Have I passed over!   40
PUTANA
Nay, what a paradise of joy have you passed under! Why, now I
commend thee, charge. Fear nothing, sweetheart: what though he
be your brother? Your brother's a man I hope, and I say still, if a
young wench feel the fit upon her, let her take anybody, father or
brother, all is one.   45
ANNABELLA
I would not have it known for all the world.
PUTANA
Nor I indeed, for the speech of the people; else 'twere
nothing.

33–4 lineation ed. (Will ... must. / When ... Soone. / Looke ... Farewell Q) The first verse line
        is incomplete, perhaps indicating a stunned pause from Annabella after Giovanni's 'I must.'
   40 *passed over* travelled through
   41 *passed under* Referring to the conventional 'missionary' sexual position, with the man
        on top of the woman.
   44 *the fit* sexual desire
   47 *the speech of the people* vulgar, censorious gossip

FLORIO   (*Within*)
Daughter Annabella!

ANNABELLA
O me, my father! [*Calls off-stage*] Here, sir! [*To* PUTANA] Reach
my work.   [PUTANA *passes her a piece of needlework*]   50

FLORIO (*Within*)
What are you doing?

ANNABELLA   So, let him come now.

Enter FLORIO, RICHARDETTO *like a doctor of physic,*
and PHILOTIS *with a lute in her hand*

FLORIO
So hard at work, that's well: you lose no time.
Look, I have brought you company: here's one,
A learned doctor, lately come from Padua,
Much skilled in physic; and for that I see
You have of late been sickly, I entreated   55
This reverend man to visit you some time.

ANNABELLA
You're very welcome, sir.

RICHARDETTO   I thank you, mistress.
Loud fame in large report hath spoke your praise
As well for virtue as perfection;   60
For which I have been bold to bring with me
A kinswoman of mine, a maid, for song
And music, one perhaps will give content.
Please you to know her?

ANNABELLA   They are parts I love,
And she for them most welcome.

---

49   s.d. *Within* Off-stage
51   s.d. *like a doctor of physic* disguised as a medical doctor (as distinct from a holder of a
       university doctorate); the disguise includes 'a broad beard' (II.vi.80), probably adopted
       the better to cover his face. Richardetto remains disguised in public until V.vi.150.
52   *lose* waste
52–7 lineation ed. (prose in Q)
54   *Padua* a city in the state of Venice, about 80 miles north east of Parma; its university
       included one of the leading medical schools in Europe. In reality, as is established in the
       next scene, Richardetto has come from the opposite direction, from Leghorn (see note
       to II.ii.75).
55   *for that* because
59   *large* extensive; full and free
64   *parts* talents, accomplishments

PHILOTIS   Thank you, lady.   65
FLORIO
Sir, now you know my house, pray make not strange;
And if you find my daughter need your art,
I'll be your paymaster.
RICHARDETTO   Sir, what I am
She shall command.
FLORIO   You shall bind me to you.
Daughter, I must have confidence with you   70
About some matters that concerns us both.
Good master Doctor, please you but walk in,
We'll crave a little of your cousin's cunning.
I think my girl hath not quite forgot
To touch an instrument; she could have done't.   75
We'll hear them both.
RICHARDETTO   I'll wait upon you, sir.   *Exeunt*

[Act II, Scene ii]

Enter SORANZO *in his study, reading a book*

SORANZO
'Love's measure is extreme, the comfort pain,

66 *make not strange* either 'don't stay away' (i.e. Florio issues a standing invitation to 'the
     Doctor'), or 'don't behave too formally'; 'strange' means 'like a stranger'
67 *art* medical skill
69 *bind . . . you* i.e. in bonds of gratitude
70 *confidence* private talk. Ford perhaps recalls the Nurse's usage in *Romeo and Juliet* (II.iii.118),
     which Shakespeare may originally have intended as a malapropism.
73 *cunning* skill
75 *touch an instrument* play a musical instrument; but 'instrument' could also mean
     'penis', so there is a bawdy undertone unintended by Florio, but relevant to the
     context now that Annabella is no longer a virgin.
     could have done used to be able to do

o   s.d. In the original production, the 'study' may have been represented by scenery set out
     in the 'discovery space' (a curtained alcove at the back of the stage). Many previous edi-
     tors assume that Soranzo writes down his poetical contradiction of Sannazaro, and supply
     a stage direction at line 9. (The first to do so was Gifford in 1827.) If so, he needs to have
     writing materials to hand, but Ford provides no attendant to carry them on for him; he
     will probably also need something to lean on as he writes. The likeliest solution is a desk
     in the 'study', probably set side-on to avoid his having to turn his back on the audience.
     Instead of a conventional entrance, he may have been 'discovered' in the study, i.e. the
     discovery space curtain would be drawn to reveal him already there.
1   s.p. SORANZO ed. (not in Q)

The life unrest, and the reward disdain.'
What's here? Look't o'er again. 'Tis so, so writes
This smooth licentious poet in his rhymes;
But Sannazar, thou liest, for had thy bosom   5
Felt such oppression as is laid on mine,
Thou wouldst have kissed the rod that made the smart.
To work then, happy Muse, and contradict
What Sannazar hath in his envy writ.
'Love's measure is the mean, sweet his annoys,   10
His pleasures life, and his reward all joys.'
Had Annabella lived when Sannazar
Did in his brief encomium celebrate
Venice, that queen of cities, he had left
That verse which gained him such a sum of gold,   15
And for one only look from Annabel
Had writ of her, and her diviner cheeks.
O, how my thoughts are –

VASQUES (*Within*)
Pray forbear! In rules of civility, let me give notice on't: I
shall be taxed of my neglect of duty and service.   20

SORANZO
What rude intrusion interrupts my peace?
Can I be nowhere private?

VASQUES (*Within*)
Troth, you wrong your modesty.

SORANZO
What's the matter, Vasques, who is't?

---

5 *Sannazar* Jacopo Sannazaro (*c.* 1456–1530), Neapolitan humanist and love poet (hence
   'licentious' in line 4). His Italian and Latin poems contain much about the pains of love,
   but nothing that corresponds precisely with the epigrammatic lines Soranzo quotes. In
   seventeenth-century England he was best known for his six-line Latin eulogy of Venice
   (*Epigrams*, I. 36), for which the city rewarded him with 600 crowns (as mentioned in
   lines 14–15).
8 *Muse* Conventionally invoked by poets as an inspiring agency; from the nine Muses of
   classical mythology, patron goddesses of the arts
9 *envy* malice
10 *mean* norm
   annoys troubles
14 *left* abandoned
20 *taxed of* reprimanded for

Enter HIPPOLITA *[dressed in black] and* VASQUES

HIPPOLITA

'Tis I: 25
Do you know me now? Look, perjured man, on her
Whom thou and thy distracted lust have wronged.
Thy sensual rage of blood hath made my youth
A scorn to men and angels; and shall I
Be now a foil to thy unsated change?   30
Thou know'st, false wanton, when my modest fame
Stood free from stain or scandal, all the charms
Of hell or sorcery could not prevail
Against the honour of my chaster bosom.
Thine eyes did plead in tears, thy tongue in oaths   35
Such, and so many, that a heart of steel
Would have been wrought to pity, as was mine;
And shall the conquest of my lawful bed,
My husband's death urged on by his disgrace,
My loss of womanhood, be ill rewarded   40
With hatred and contempt? No! Know, Soranzo,
I have a spirit doth as much distaste
The slavery of fearing thee as thou
Dost loathe the memory of what hath passed.

SORANZO

Nay, dear Hippolita –

HIPPOLITA   Call me not dear,   45
Nor think with supple words to smooth the grossness
Of my abuses. 'Tis not your new mistress,
Your goodly Madam Merchant, shall triumph
On my dejection: tell her thus from me,
My birth was nobler, and by much more free.   50

---

28 *rage of blood* lustful frenzy
30 *foil . . . unsated change* A foil is a thin sheet of metal on which a jewel is mounted to set
    off its lustre by contrast; Hippolita is saying that, having changed lovers even though his
    sexual appetite is not 'sated' (fully satisfied), Soranzo now uses her as the foil to his new
    love, Annabella.
39 *urged on* partly induced
40 *womanhood* womanly attributes (here, sexual fidelity to her husband)
42 *distaste* dislike
48 *Madam Merchant* Annabella; Florio is either a merchant or a member of the merchant
    class, which is socially lower than Hippolita's.
48–9 *triumph . . . dejection* exult in my being humiliated
50 *free* honourable

SORANZO

You are too violent.

HIPPOLITA   You are too double
In your dissimulation. Seest thou this,
This habit, these black mourning weeds of care?
'Tis thou art cause of this, and hast divorced
My husband from his life and me from him,   55
And made me widow in my widowhood.

SORANZO

Will you yet hear?

HIPPOLITA   More of thy perjuries?
Thy soul is drowned too deeply in those sins:
Thou need'st not add to th'number.

SORANZO   Then I'll leave you;
You are past all rules of sense.

HIPPOLITA   And thou of grace.   60

VASQUES

Fie, mistress, you are not near the limits of reason: if my lord
had a resolution as noble as virtue itself, you take the course to
unedge it all. Sir, I beseech you do not perplex her. Griefs, alas,
will have a vent; I dare undertake Madam Hippolita will now
freely hear you.   65

SORANZO

Talk to a woman frantic! Are these the fruits of your
love?

---

51 *double* duplicitous
53 *weeds* clothes
56 *widow in my widowhood* doubly a widow, both because her husband is dead and because
    Soranzo has not kept his promise to be her second husband (see below, lines 69–71)
63 *unedge* make blunt (like a sword)
    perplex torment
64 *will . . . vent* must be spoken
65 *freely* without interrupting
66–7 *Are . . . love?* This could be spoken to either Vasques or Hippolita, but in either case it
    carries implications about Soranzo's relationship with the former. If to Vasques, it means
    'Is your love to me so unprofitable that I end up having to reason with a deranged
    woman?', and it is suggestive that he speaks not of Vasques' duty but his love (implying
    a more personal relationship than is usual between master and servant, though not nec-
    essarily a sexual one). If he is speaking to Hippolita, however, it means 'So this is how
    your love for me ends up', with a kind of forced reasonableness that is obviously crass in
    the circumstances; in this case, the whole line shows him first rejecting and then sub-
    mitting to Vasques' recommendation, suggesting the servant's unusually dominant role
    in their relationship.

[75]

HIPPOLITA
    They are the fruits of thy untruth, false man!
    Didst thou not swear, whilst yet my husband lived,
    That thou wouldst wish no happiness on earth   70
    More than to call me wife? Didst thou not vow,
    When he should die, to marry me? For which
    The devil in my blood, and thy protests,
    Caused me to counsel him to undertake
    A voyage to Leghorn, for that we heard   75
    His brother there was dead and left a daughter
    Young and unfriended, who with much ado
    I wished him to bring hither. He did so,
    And went, and, as thou know'st, died on the way.
    Unhappy man to buy his death so dear   80
    With my advice! Yet thou for whom I did it
    Forget'st thy vows, and leav'st me to my shame.
SORANZO
    Who could help this?
HIPPOLITA   Who? Perjured man, thou couldst,
    If thou hadst faith or love.
SORANZO   You are deceived:
    The vows I made, if you remember well,   85
    Were wicked and unlawful, 'twere more sin
    To keep them than to break them; as for me,
    I cannot mask my penitence. Think thou
    How much thou hast digressed from honest shame
    In bringing of a gentleman to death   90
    Who was thy husband. Such a one as he,
    So noble in his quality, condition,
    Learning, behaviour, entertainment, love,
    As Parma could not show a braver man.

73 *protests* solemn affirmations, vows (to marry her)
75 *Leghorn* a coastal town in Tuscany (after 1606, a city) about 80 miles south of Parma; the
     journey between the two would take a traveller through dangerous mountain districts.
77 *unfriended* with nobody to support her
89 *digressed . . . shame* deviated from proper behaviour (inhibited from wrongdoing by
     shame); Hippolita is now 'shameless'
92 *quality* social position or personal disposition
     condition personal qualities
93 *entertainment* hospitality (considered a mark of nobility)
94 *braver* finer

VASQUES
 You do not well, this was not your promise.   95
SORANZO
 I care not: let her know her monstrous life.
 Ere I'll be servile to so black a sin
 I'll be a corpse. Woman, come here no more,
 Learn to repent and die; for by my honour
 I hate thee and thy lust. You have been too foul. *[Exit]* 100
VASQUES
 This part has been scurvily played.
HIPPOLITA
 How foolishly this beast contemns his fate,
 And shuns the use of that which I more scorn
 Than I once loved, his love! But let him go:
 My vengeance shall give comfort to his woe.   105
        She offers to go away
VASQUES
 Mistress, mistress, Madam Hippolita! Pray, a word or two.
HIPPOLITA
 With me, sir?
VASQUES
 With you if you please.
HIPPOLITA
 What is't?
VASQUES
 I know you are infinitely moved now, and you think you 110
 have cause: some I confess you have, but, sure, not so much
 as you imagine.
HIPPOLITA
 Indeed!
VASQUES
 O you were miserably bitter, which you followed even to
 the last syllable; faith, you were somewhat too shrewd. By 115
 my life, you could not have took my lord in a worse time
 since I first knew him; tomorrow you shall find him a
 new man.

---

102 *contemns* contemptuously disregards, scorns
105 *his woe* the woe he has caused her
114 *followed* maintained
115 *shrewd* aggressively harsh, scolding

HIPPOLITA
Well, I shall wait his leisure.

VASQUES
Fie, this is not a hearty patience: it comes sourly from you.   120
Troth, let me persuade you for once.

HIPPOLITA
[*Aside*] I have it, and it shall be so. Thanks opportunity!
[*To him*] Persuade me to what?

VASQUES
Visit him in some milder temper. O, if you could but master a little your female spleen, how might you win him!   125

HIPPOLITA
He will never love me. Vasques, thou hast been a too trusty servant to such a master, and I believe thy reward in the end will fall
out like mine.

VASQUES
So perhaps too.

HIPPOLITA
Resolve thyself, it will. Had I one so true, so truly honest,   130
so secret to my counsels, as thou hast been to him and his, I should
think it a slight acquittance not only to make him master of all I
have, but even of myself.

VASQUES
O, you are a noble gentlewoman!

HIPPOLITA
Wilt thou feed always upon hopes? Well, I know thou art wise, and   135
seest the reward of an old servant daily what it is.

VASQUES
Beggary and neglect.

HIPPOLITA
True; but Vasques, wert thou mine, and wouldst be private to me
and my designs, I here protest myself, and all what I can else call
mine, should be at thy dispose.   140

120   *hearty* sincere, heartfelt
125   *spleen* bitter passion
131   *and his* Probably referring to Vasques' prior relationship with Soranzo's dead father (see
        V.vi.115–18).
132   *acquittance* repayment
132–133   *master . . . of myself* her husband
139   *all what* everything
140   *dispose* disposal

VASQUES

[Aside] Work you that way, old mole? Then I have the wind of you.
[To her] I were not worthy of it, by any desert that could lie within
my compass. If I could –

HIPPOLITA

What then?

VASQUES

I should then hope to live in these my old years with rest and   145
security.

HIPPOLITA

Give me thy hand. Now promise but thy silence,
And help to bring to pass a plot I have,
And here in sight of Heaven, that being done,
I make thee lord of me and mine estate.   150

VASQUES

Come, you are merry: this is such a happiness that I can neither
think or believe.

HIPPOLITA

Promise thy secrecy, and 'tis confirmed.

VASQUES

Then here I call our good genii for witnesses, whatsoever
your designs are, or against whomsoever, I will not only   155
be a special actor therein, but never disclose it till it be
effected.

141   *mole* Vasques imagines Hippolita's plotting in terms of a mole's underground burrow-
      ing; but a relevant secondary sense alludes to the animal's supposed blindness (as Hippolita
      is blind to Vasques' own motives).

141   *I have . . . you* Vasques describes himself in terms of a predator upwind of its prey
      (= Hippolita), and so able to track it by scent.

147   *Give me thy hand* This may mean more than simply shaking hands on a bargain:
      since the joining of hands also had a specific matrimonial significance (see note to III.vi.52
      s.d.) which is activated by the terms of Hippolita's offer to Vasques, it also underlines
      how absolutely they have committed themselves to each other in and through the plot
      against Soranzo.

151–2   prose ed. (Come . . . merry, / This . . . can / Neither . . . beleeue Q)

151   *merry* only joking

154   *good genii* guardian angels; Ford had probably read in Robert Burton's *Anatomy of Melan-
      choly* (1621) that 'every man hath a good and a bad angel attending of him in particular
      all his life', and that these spirits were known as *genii* (Clarendon edn.,
      1989–, vol. 1, p. 191).
      for witnesses ed. (foe-witnesses Q)

HIPPOLITA
    I take thy word, and with that, thee for mine.
    Come then, let's more confer of this anon.
    On this delicious bane my thoughts shall banquet;   160
    Revenge shall sweeten what my griefs have tasted.   *Exeunt*

[Act II, Scene iii]

Enter RICHARDETTO *and* PHILOTIS

RICHARDETTO
    Thou seest, my lovely niece, these strange mishaps,
    How all my fortunes turn to my disgrace,
    Wherein I am but as a looker-on
    Whiles others act my shame and I am silent.
PHILOTIS
    But, uncle, wherein can this borrowed shape   5
    Give you content?
RICHARDETTO   I'll tell thee, gentle niece:
    Thy wanton aunt in her lascivious riots
    Lives now secure, thinks I am surely dead
    In my late journey to Leghorn for you,
    As I have caused it to be rumoured out.   10
    Now would I see with what an impudence
    She gives scope to her loose adultery,
    And how the common voice allows hereof:
    Thus far I have prevailed.

160 *bane* poison

  0 s.d. It is possible that Richardetto does not wear his disguise in private with Philotis.
      If so, the costume and false beard need to be seen on stage in this scene, not only
      because Philotis refers to the disguise ('this borrowed shape') in line 5 but also to show
      the audience that this is the same character as the Doctor who appeared in II.i (rather
      than the same actor doubling another role). He might, for example, be taking off the
      beard as he enters (in which case he will need to put it hastily back on when Grimaldi
      arrives later in the scene).
  4 *act my shame* Because in reality Richardetto is planning revenge, his 'shame' (as an
      unavenged cuckold) is only a fiction in which other people unwittingly participate, like
      actors performing a play.
  8 *secure* unsuspecting, with a false sense of security.
 13 *how . . . allows* how public opinion responds

PHILOTIS   Alas, I fear
You mean some strange revenge.
RICHARDETTO   O, be not troubled: 15
Your ignorance shall plead for you in all.
But to our business: what, you learnt for certain
How Signor Florio means to give his daughter
In marriage to Soranzo?
PHILOTIS   Yes, for certain.
RICHARDETTO
But how find you young Annabella's love   20
Inclined to him?
PHILOTIS   For aught I could perceive,
She neither fancies him or any else.
RICHARDETTO
There's mystery in that which time must show.
She used you kindly?
PHILOTIS   Yes.
RICHARDETTO   And craved your company?
PHILOTIS
Often.
RICHARDETTO   'Tis well: it goes as I could wish.   25
I am the Doctor now, and, as for you,
None knows you; if all fail not we shall thrive.
But who comes here?

Enter GRIMALDI

I know him: 'tis Grimaldi,
A Roman and a soldier, near allied
Unto the Duke of Monferrato; one   30

16   Richardetto saves her from becoming an accessory in his criminal plans (and so legally
     liable for them) by not telling her what they are.
18   *How* That
24   *used* behaved towards, treated
28   s–d. Q places Grimaldi's entrance here, but it is hard to make sense of this in staging the
     scene: it seems to indicate that Grimaldi walks uninvited and unannounced into what
     the preceding dialogue suggests to be Richardetto's private chamber, a discourtesy the
     audience would be particularly likely to notice after Hippohta's bursting in on Soranzo
     in the previous scene; he is then ignored for six lines while Richardetto explains who he
     is. Possibly Richardetto's 'Who comes here?' is in response to a knock at the door; he
     would then look through a spy-hole or lattice in the door to see the caller, talk briefly to
     Philotis about him (perhaps while donning his disguise; see note to 0 s.d.), and then
     open the door tor Grimaldi to enter after line 33.

Attending on the Nuncio of the Pope
That now resides in Parma, by which means
He hopes to get the love of Annabella.

GRIMALDI
Save you, sir.

RICHARDETTO And you, sir.

GRIMALDI   I have heard
Of your approvèd skill, which through the city   35
Is freely talked of, and would crave your aid.

RICHARDETTO
For what, sir?

GRIMALDI   Marry sir, for this –
But I would speak in private.

RICHARDETTO   Leave us, cousin.

                                        Exit PHILOTIS

GRIMALDI
I love fair Annabella, and would know
Whether in arts there may not be receipts   40
To move affection.

RICHARDETTO   Sir, perhaps there may,
But these will nothing profit you.

GRIMALDI   Not me?

RICHARDETTO
Unless I be mistook, you are a man
Greatly in favour with the Cardinal.

GRIMALDI
What of that?

RICHARDETTO In duty to his grace,   45
I will be bold to tell you, if you seek
To marry Florio's daughter, you must first
Remove a bar 'twixt you and her.

GRIMALDI   Who's that?

---

31 *Nuncio* a permanent representative of the Pope at a foreign court, with both political
and ecclesiastical powers

32 *by whlch means* i.e. by playing on his association with an influential person

34 *save you* a greeting (worn down from 'God save you')

40 *arts* Grimaldi's unusual plural is perhaps intended to flatter Richardetto with omni-
competence. Dyce and some other editors, suspecting a misprint, emend to 'art'.

40–1 *receipts . . . affection* love-philtres ('receipts' = recipes)

RICHARDETTO
  Soranzo is the man that hath her heart,
  And while he lives, be sure you cannot speed.   50
GRIMALDI
  Soranzo! What, mine enemy, is't he?
RICHARDETTO
  Is he your enemy?
GRIMALDI   The man I hate
  Worse than confusion. I'll kill him straight.
RICHARDETTO
  Nay, then, take mine advice:
  Even for his grace's sake the Cardinal,   55
  I'll find a time when he and she do meet,
  Of which I'll give you notice, and to be sure
  He shall not 'scape you, I'll provide a poison
  To dip your rapier's point in: if he had
  As many heads as Hydra had, he dies.   60
GRIMALDI
  But shall I trust thee, Doctor?
RDETTO   As yourself,
  Doubt not in aught. [*Aside*] Thus shall the fates decree,
  By me Soranzo falls, that ruined me.   *Exeunt*

[Act II, Scene iv]

Enter DONADO [*with a letter*], BERGETTO *and* POGGIO

DONADO
  Well sir, I must be content to be both your secretary and your mes-
  senger myself: I cannot tell what this letter may work, but as sure

50 *speed* succeed
53 lineation ed. (Worse . . . Confusion; / I'le . . . streight Q)
55 This line (presented as a parenthesis in Q) could qualify either the preceding or, as here
    punctuated, the following line. In the former case, Richardetto presumptuously recom-
    mends that Grimaldi should accept his advice for the Cardinal's sake; in the latter, he
    offers to help plan the murder as a favour to the Cardinal through Grimaldi, reflecting
    not only his disingenuous humility in the rest of the exchange but also his facade of not
    being personally concerned in the crime.
59–60 *if he . . . Hydra had* no matter how hard he is to kill. The Hydra was a many-headed venomous
    monster in classical mythology, which grew two new heads for every one that was cut off.

1 *secretary* Donado has written the letter himself.

as I am alive, if thou come once to talk with her, I fear thou wilt
mar whatsoever I make.

BERGETTO

You 'make', uncle? Why, am not I big enough to carry mine own   5
letter, I pray?

DONADO

Ay, ay, carry a fool's head o'thy own. Why thou dunce, wouldst
thou write a letter, and carry it thyself?

BERGETTO

Yes, that I would, and read it to her with my own mouth; for you
must think, if she will not believe me myself when she hears me   10
speak, she will not believe another's handwriting. O, you think I
am a blockhead, uncle! No, sir, Poggio knows I have indited a letter myself, so I have.

POGGIO

Yes truly, sir, I have it in my pocket.

DONADO

A sweet one no doubt, pray let's see't.   15

[POGGIO *gives* BERGETTO *the letter*]

BERGETTO

I cannot read my own hand very well, Poggio. Read it,
Poggio.

DONADO

Begin.

POGGIO (*Reads*)

'Most dainty and honey-sweet mistress, I could call you
fair, and lie as fast as any that loves you; but my uncle being   20
the elder man, I leave it to him as more fit for his age and
the colour of his beard. I am wise enough to tell you I can
board where I see occasion: or if you like my uncle's wit better than

---

7   *a fool's . . . own* Proverbial (Tilley, G. 519).

12   *indited* composed

16   *hand* handwriting

16   prose ed. (I . . . *Poggio*, / Reads . . . *Poggio* Q)

20   *fast* firmly, utterly

22   *the colour of his beard* Probably just a periphrasis for age; it is tempting to suppose a latent
       pun on 'white lie', but *OED* does not record the term in use before 1741.

23   *board* 'chat up', make sexual advances (to Annabella); an alternative might be
       'bourd' (= jest)
       occasion opportunity
       or either (= 'on the one hand')

mine, you shall marry me; if you like mine better than his,
I will marry you in spite of your teeth; so commending my best   25
parts to you, I rest
    Yours upwards and downwards, or you may choose,
                              Bergetto.'

BERGETTO
Ah, ha! Here's stuff, uncle!

DONADO
Here's stuff indeed to shame us all. Pray whose advice did you take   30
in this learned letter?

POGGIO
None, upon my word, but mine own.

BERGETTO
And mine, uncle, believe it nobody's else; 'twas mine own brain,
I thank a good wit fot't.

DONADO
Get you home, sir, and look you keep within doors till I   35
return.

BERGETTO
How! That were a jest indeed; I scorn it i 'faith.

DONADO
What, you do not!

BERGETTO
Judge me, but I do now.

POGGIO
Indeed, sir, 'tis very unhealthy.   40

DONADO
Well, sir, if I hear any of your apish running to motions and fop-
peries till I come back, you were as good no: look to't.   *Exit*

BERGETTO
Poggio, shall's steal to see this horse with the head in's tail?

25 *in spite of your teeth* whether you like it or not (literally, notwithstanding your resist-
    ance)
30–1 prose ed. (Here's . . . all, / Pray . . . Letter? Q)
40 Probably addressed to Donado (Poggio usually calls Bergetto 'master' rather than 'sir').
41 *apish* foolish (literally, like a monkey imitating a human being)
    motions puppet-shows
42 *you . . . no* you'll regret it (literally, you had better not have done so)

POGGIO
Ay, but you must take heed of whipping.
BERGETTO
Dost take me for a child, Poggio? Come, honest Poggio.   45

Exeunt

[Act II, Scene v]

Enter FRIAR *and* GIOVANNI

FRIAR
Peace! Thou hast told a tale whose every word
Threatens eternal slaughter to the soul;
I'm sorry I have heard it. Would mine ears
Had been one minute deaf before the hour
That thou camest to me! O young man cast away,   5
By the religious number of mine order,
I day and night have waked my agèd eyes
Above my strength, to weep on thy behalf;
But Heaven is angry, and be thou resolved,
Thou art a man remarked to taste a mischief.   10
Look for't: though it come late, it will come sure.
GIOVANNI
Father, in this you are uncharitable.
What I have done I'll prove both fit and good:
It is a principle, which you have taught
When I was yet your scholar, that the frame   15
And composition of the mind doth follow
The frame and composition of the body;
So where the body's furniture is beauty,

---

44 *take . . . whipping* beware beating (as a punishment for disobedience)
45 prose ed. (Dost . . . *Poggio,* / Come . . . *Poggio* Q)

4 *one . . . hour* struck deaf the moment before the time
5 *cast away* damned (literally, discarded)
6 *number* company, group of people
10 *remarked* marked out
12 *uncharitable* lacking in Christian love for one's fellow men (see also note on *charity*, IV.i.56)
15 *frame* ed. (Fame Q)
18 *furniture* accoutrement

The mind's must needs be virtue; which allowed,
Virtue itself is reason but refined,   20
And love the quintessence of that; this proves
My sister's beauty, being rarely fair,
Is rarely virtuous; chiefly in her love,
And chiefly in that love, her love to me;
If hers to me, then so is mine to her;   25
Since in like causes are effects alike.

FRIAR

O ignorance in knowledge! Long ago,
How often have I warned thee this before!
Indeed, if we were sure there were no Deity,
Nor heaven nor hell, then to be led alone   30
By Nature's light – as were philosophers
Of elder times – might instance some defence;
But 'tis not so. Then, madman, thou wilt find
That Nature is in Heaven's positions blind.

GIOVANNI

Your age o'errules you; had you youth like mine,   35
You'd make her love your heaven, and her divine.

FRIAR

Nay, then I see thou'rt too far sold to hell;
It lie's not in the compass of my prayers
To call thee back. Yet let me counsel thee:
Persuade thy sister to some marriage.   40

GIOVANNI

Marriage? Why, that's to damn her: that's to prove
Her greedy of variety of lust.

FRIAR

O fearful! If thou wilt not, give me leave
To shrive her, lest she should die unabsolved.

---

21 *quintessence* a stage of refinement beyond essence; hence, the purest manifestation
30–2 *led alone . . . times* guided by empirical reasoning alone, without the benefit of divine
revelation, like the pre-Christian Greek philosophers
34 *Nature . . . blind* empiricism ('Nature') is ignorant about the 'positions' affirmed by God;
'positions' usually meant statements for academic disputation, but the Friar's point is
that God's 'positions' are not debatable but absolute.
41–2 If she marries, Annabella will show herself not to be satisfied with the one man she already
has; this desire for multiple lovers ('variety of lusts') will be unchaste and so will damn
her.
44 *shrive her* hear her confession and grant her absolution of her sins

GIOVANNI
   At your best leisure, father; then she'll tell you   45
   How dearly she doth prize my matchless love.
   Then you will know what pity 'twere we two
   Should have been sundered from each other's arms.
   View well her face, and in that little round
   You may observe a world of variety: 50
   For colour, lips, for sweet perfumes, her breath;
   For jewels, eyes; for threads of purest gold,
   Hair; for delicious choice of flowers, cheeks;
   Wonder in every portion of that throne.
   Hear her but speak, and you will swear the spheres   55
   Make music to the citizens in heaven;
   But father, what is else for pleasure framed
   Lest I offend your ears shall go unnamed.

FRIAR
   The more I hear, I pity thee the more,
   That one so excellent should give those parts   60
   All to a second death. What I can do
   Is but to pray; and yet I could advise thee,
   Wouldst thou be ruled.

GIOVANNI   In what?

FRIAR   Why, leave her yet.
   The throne of mercy is above your trespass;
   Yet time is left you both –

GIOVANNI   To embrace each other;   65
   Else let all time be struck quite out of number.

49–58 This passage draws on the Renaissance poetic form of the blazon, which described a
     woman in a catalogue of her beauties from head to toe.
  54 *throne* Giovanni treats his sister with the veneration due to God or a king.
  55 *the spheres* In the Ptolemaic theory of the universe, between Earth and heaven there were
     seven planets (including the sun and moon) fixed to concentric crystal spheres; their
     harmonious rotation was thought to produce a beautiful melody.
  57 *what . . . framed* Annabella's private parts; Giovanni is heterodox in saying that they were
     created by God ('framed') for pleasure rather than procreation.
  60 *parts* abilities, skills
  61 *a second death* damnation
  62 *but* only
  64 God's power to exercise mercy is greater than the sin Giovanni and Annabella have com-
     mitted; in Christian theology, all sins except despair of mercy can be forgiven if the sinner
     repents.
  65 *Yet* Still
  66 *number* sequence

She is like me, and I like her resolved.

FRIAR

No more: I'll visit her. This grieves me most,
Things being thus, a pair of souls are lost.   *Exeunt*

[Act II, Scene vi]

Enter FLORIO, DONADO, ANNABELLA, PUTANA

FLORIO

Where's Giovanni?

ANNABELLA   Newly walked abroad,
And, as I heard him say, gone to the Friar,
His reverend tutor.

FLORIO   That's a blessèd man,
A man made up of holiness; I hope
He'll teach him how to gain another world.   5

DONADO

Fair gentlewoman, here's a letter sent
To you from my young cousin. I dare swear
He loves you in his soul; would you could hear
Sometimes what I see daily, sighs and tears,
As if his breast were prison to his heart!   10

FLORIO

Receive it, Annabella.

ANNABELLA   Alas, good man!
                    [*She takes the letter, but does not read it*]

DONADO

What's that she said?

PUTANA

An't please you, sir, she said, 'Alas, good man!' [*Aside to* DONADO]
Truly, I do commend him to her every night before her first sleep,

---

5 *gain another world* achieve a place in heaven

7 *cousin* kinsman

11 s.d. It is unclear when Annabella opens the letter; inside it she will find the jewel mentioned at I.iii.81.

14 *first sleep* sleep during the first part of the night (after which a person might wake and take drink before sleeping again). The first sleep was thought to be associated with dreams, especially, in young women, erotic ones; compare Lording Barry, *Ram Alley*, 1483–6: 'When maids awaked from their first sleep, / Deceived with dreams, began to weep / And think, if dreams such pleasures know, / What sport the substance then would show.'

because I would have her dream of him; and she hearkens to that   15
most religiously.

DONADO

[*Aside to* PUTANA] Say'st so? Godamercy, Putana, there's
something for thee, [*Gives her money*] and prithee do what
thou canst on his behalf; sha' not be lost labour, take my
word for't.   20

PUTANA

[*Aside to* DONADO] Thank you most heartily, sir; now I have a feeling of your mind, let me alone to work.

ANNABELLA

Guardian!

PUTANA

Did you call?

ANNABELLA

Keep this letter.   25

DONADO

Signor Florio, in any case bid her read it instantly.

FLORIO

Keep it, for what? Pray read it me here right.

ANNABELLA

I shall, sir.   *She reads*

DONADO

How d'ee find her inclined, signor?

FLORIO

Troth sir, I know not how; not all so well   30
As I could wish.

ANNABELLA

Sir, I am bound to rest your cousin's debtor.
The jewel I'll return; for if he love,
I'll count that love a jewel.

---

17 *Godamercy* Thank you
18 *prithee* please
22 *feeling . . . mind* understanding of your intentions (punning on the tangible reward she
    has just received)
27 *read it me* oblige me by reading it (silently), *not* read it (aloud) to me; Florio uses the
    grammatical inflection known as the ethical dative, common in the seventeenth century
    but now obsolete, which is used to imply indirect involvement in an action.
    here right straight away

DONADO   Mark you that?
Nay, keep them both, sweet maid.
ANNABELLA   You must excuse me: 35
Indeed I will not keep it.
FLORIO   Where's the ring,
That which your mother in her will bequeathed,
And charged you on her blessing not to give't
To any but your husband? Send back that.
ANNABELLA
I have it not.
FLORIO   Ha! 'Have it not', where is't?   40
ANNABELLA
My brother in the morning took it from me,
Said he would wear't today.
FLORIO   Well, what do you say
To young Bergetto's love? Are you content
To match with him? Speak.
DONADO   There's the point indeed.
ANNABELLA
[*Aside*] What shall I do? I must say something now.   45
FLORIO
What say? Why d'ee not speak?
ANNABELLA   Sir, with your leave;
Please you to give me freedom.
FLORIO   Yes you have't.
ANNABELLA
Signor Donado, it your nephew mean
To raise his better fortunes in his match,
The hope of me will hinder such a hope.   50
Sir, if you love him, as I know you do,

36–9 Perhaps Florio infers from Annabella's polite words (lines 32–4) that she is genuinely
      interested in Bergetto.
44 *match* marry
46 *What say?* What do you say?
47 *Please . . . freedom* Punctuation as in Q; some other editors (beginning with Gifford in
    1827) end the line with a question mark. This is not a necessary intervention, since
    Annabella may be using 'please' in the sense *OED* 3c, implying 'May it please you'; its
    effect is to make her appear less forward, more uncertain with her father than if, as here
    and in Q, the line is played as a statement. *have't* ed. (haue Q)
50 i.e. he is wasting his time

Find one more worthy of his choice than me;
In short, I'm sure I sha' not be his wife.

DONADO

Why, here's plain dealing; I commend thee for't,
And all the worst I wish thee, is Heaven bless thee!   55
Your father yet and I will still be friends,
Shall we not, Signor Florio?

FLORIO   Yes, why not?

Enter BERGETTO *and* POGGIO

Look, here your cousin comes.

DONADO

[*Aside*] O coxcomb, what doth he make here?

BERGETTO

Where's my uncle, sirs?   60

DONADO

What's the news now?

BERGETTO

Save you, uncle, save you. You must not think I come for nothing,
masters; and how, and how is't? What, you have read my letter?
Ah, there I – tickled you i' faith!

POGGIO

But 'twere better you had tickled her in another place.   65

BERGETTO

Sirrah! [*To* ANNABELLA] Sweetheart, I'll tell thee a good jest, and
riddle what 'tis.

---

54 *plain dealing* frank honesty
57 s.d. ed.; after line 58 in Q
59 *what . . . here?* what's he doing here?
60 *sirs* This must be addressed to Florio and Donado, the only two men already on stage
    when Bergetto and Poggio enter; probably the scene should be staged in such a way that
    Bergetto cannot initially see Donado's face.
64 *I – tickled* Q's dash may be intended to indicate inarticulacy, as Bergetto gropes for the
    right word.
65–6 *But . . . Sweetheart* This passage is open to many different interpretations in performance;
    which is chosen will depend on the director's and actors' broader understanding of the
    two characters and the relationship between them. If 'Sirrah' is taken to be spoken to Pog-
    gio, as punctuated here, then Poggio's preceding remark can be spoken aloud; Bergetto's
    response need not mean that he recognizes the inappropriateness of the bawdy reference
    to heavy petting – he could just be irritated at the interruption. Other editors take Q's 'Sir-
    rah *Sweetheart*' to be an inept form of address to Annabella, and accordingly make Poggio's
    line an aside, either spoken to Bergetto (Dyce) or directly to the audience (Lomax).
67 *riddle* guess

ANNABELLA

You say you'd tell me.

BERGETTO

As I was walking just now in the street, I met a swaggering
fellow would needs take the wall of me; and because he did   70
thrust me, I very valiantly called him rogue. He hereupon
bade me draw. I told him I had more wit than so; but when
he saw that I would not, he did so maul me with the hilts
of his rapier, that my head sung whilst my feet capered in
the kennel.   75

DONADO

[*Aside*] Was ever the like ass seen?

ANNABELLA

And what did you all this while?

BERGETTO

Laugh at him for a gull, till I see the blood run about mine ears,
and then I could not choose but find in my heart to cry till a fellow with a broad beard – they say he is a newcome doctor – called   80
me into this house, and gave me a plaster – look you, here 'tis –
and, sir, there was a young wench washed my face and hands most
excellently; i'faith I shall love her as long as I live for't. Did she not,
Poggio?

POGGIO

Yes, and kissed him too.   85

---

70   *take . . . me* The ruffian forced Bergetto away from the wall and towards the middle of
the street. The preferred walking position in seventeenth-century city streets was along-
side the wall, because the drainage gutter or 'kennel' ran down the middle, making that
part of the street not only wet but filthy; it was considered polite to step aside from the
wall for someone of higher rank than yourself, whereas 'taking the wall' was considered
offensive and sometimes provoked street-fights.

73   *hilts* Probably a colloquial rather than an ignorant usage, though it is not recorded in
OED.

78   *gull* fool

81   *here 'tis* This moment is open to two distinct stagings, depending on whether or not
Bergetto's 'plaster' (a bandage, larger than a modern band-aid) is already visible to the
audience and characters. Nobody remarks on it when he enters (unless this is a latent secondary meaning of Donado's 'coxcomb' in line 59), which might be out of politeness or
might be because they actually cannot see it. In the latter case Bergetto is probably wearing a hat, which he now removes to show the bandage. Alternatively, 'here 'tis' could
be played as a comically fatuous line drawing attention to something that is already
obvious.

BERGETTO

Why la now, you think I tell a lie, uncle, I warrant.

DONADO

Would he that beat thy blood out of thy head had beaten some wit
into it, for I fear thou never wilt have any.

BERGETTO

O, uncle, but there was a wench would have done a man's heart
good to have looked on her. By this light, she had a face methinks   90
worth twenty of you, Mistress Annabella.

DONADO

[*Aside*] Was ever such a fool born?

ANNABELLA

I am glad she liked you, sir.

BERGETTO

Are you so? By my troth, I thank you, forsooth.

FLORIO

Sure 'twas the Doctor's niece that was last day with us here.   95

BERGETTO

'Twas she, 'twas she!

DONADO

How do you know that, simplicity?

BERGETTO

Why, does not he say so? If I should have said no, I should have
given him the lie, uncle, and so have deserved a dry beating again:
I'll none of that.   100

FLORIO

A very modest, well-behaved young maid as I have seen.

DONADO

Is she indeed?

FLORIO

Indeed she is, if I have any judgement.

DONADO

Well, sir, now you are free: you need not care for sending

---

86   *la now* an emphatic expression with no particular meaning

89   *O, uncle* This could be played either as an indication of Bergetto's irrepressibility (as
punctuated here) or a response to Donado's previous comment ('O uncle!').

93   *liked* pleased

99   *given . . . the lie* To tell someone they were lying ('give the lie') was a grave insult which
usually led to a duel.
     dry hard, severe

103 lineation ed. (Indeed / Shee . . . Judgement Q)

letters now, you are dismissed; your mistress here will none   105
of you.

BERGETTO

No? Why, what care I for that? I can have wenches enough in Parma
for half-a-crown apiece, cannot I, Poggio?

POGGIO

I'll warrant you, sir.

DONADO

Signor Florio,   110
I thank you for your free recourse you gave
For my admittance; and to you, fair maid,
That jewel I will give you 'gainst your marriage.
[*To* BERGETTO] Come, will you go, sir?

BERGETTO

Ay, marry will I. Mistress, farewell, mistress; I'll come again tomor-   115
row; farewell, mistress.

        Exeunt DONADO, BERGETTO, *and* POGGIO

        Enter GIOVANNI

FLORIO

Son where have you been? What, alone, alone, still, still?
I would not have it so: you must forsake
This over-bookish humour. Well, your sister
Hath shook the fool off.

GIOVANNI   'Twas no match for her.   120

FLORIO

'Twas not indeed, I meant it nothing less.
Soranzo is the man I only like:
Look on him, Annabella! Come, 'tis supper-time,
And it grows late.   *Exit*

---

108 *half-a-crown apiece* Half-a-crown (2*s*. 6*d*.) was about twice the going rate for prostitutes
     in mid-seventeenth-century England; Bergetto is probably not speaking from experi-
     ence.

110–14 lineation ed. (prose in Q)

111 *recourse* access

113 *'gainst* in anticipation of (with the expectation that the jewel will be worn on the wed-
     ding day, hence Giovanni's reaction at line 128)

117–20 *Son . . . off* lineation ed. (prose in Q)

119 *humour* quirk of personality

120 *match* appropriate marriage

122 *the man . . . like* my preferred candidate among the suitors

GIOVANNI

Whose jewel's that?   125

ANNABELLA

Some sweetheart's.

GIOVANNI   So I think.

ANNABELLA   A lusty youth,

Signor Donado, gave it me to wear

Against my marriage.

GIOVANNI   But you shall not wear it:

Send it him back again.

ANNABELLA   What, you are jealous?

GIOVANNI

That you shall know anon, at better leisure.   130

Welcome, sweet night! The evening crowns the day.

Exeunt

Act III [Scene i]

Enter BERGETTO *and* POGGIO

BERGETTO

Does my uncle think to make me a baby still? No, Poggio, he shall

know I have a sconce now.

POGGIO

Ay, let him not bob you off like an ape with an apple.

125–31 Putana is still present on stage during this exchange.

126–7 *A lusty . . . Donado* The passage is open to two distinct interpretations. As punctuated here, Annabella ironically calls old Donado a youth, expecting Giovanni's complicity in the joke and not yet recognizing how far the gift of the ring has irritated him. Alternatively, 'a lusty youth' could be the teasing fiction and 'Signor Donado' the harmless truth; this interpretation requires a stronger pause after 'youth', in which her playfulness evaporates as she realizes she may have gone too far.

126–9 *A . . . again* lineation ed. (A . . . me / To . . . Marriage. /But . . . againe Q)

2 *sconce* brain, intellect (literally, head)

3 *let . . . apple* don't let him make a fool of you. To bob someone off was to get rid of them (fob them off) with a trifling bribe, as an ape will be easily satisfied with an apple (supposedly its favourite food; bananas were little known in England at the time).

BERGETTO

'Sfoot, I will have the wench, if he were ten uncles, in despite of
his nose, Poggio.   5

POGGIO

Hold him to the grindstone, and give not a jot of ground: she hath
in a manner promised you already.

BERGETTO

True, Poggio, and her uncle the Doctor swore I should marry
her.

POGGIO

He swore, I remember.   10

BERGETTO

And I will have her, that's more. Didst see the codpiece-point she
gave me, and the box of marmalade?

POGGIO

Very well, and kissed you, that my chops watered at the
sight on't. There's no way but to clap up a marriage in hugger-
mugger.   15

BERGETTO

I will do't, for I tell thee, Poggio, I begin to grow valiant, methinks,
and my courage begins to rise.

POGGIO

Should you be afraid of your uncle?

BERGETTO

Hang him, old doting rascal, no: I say I will have her.

POGGIO

Lose no time, then.   20

---

 4 *'Sfoot* a strong oath, contracted from 'by God's foot'
     the wench Philotis, not Annabella
6–9 prose ed. (Hold . . . ground, / Shee . . . already. / True . . .' . . . Doctor / Swore . . . her Q)
 8 s.p. BERGETTO ed. (line attributed to Poggio in Q)
11 *codpiece-point* a lace for fastening a codpiece (a decorative pouch worn by a man over
     his genitals; no longer fashionable when the play was written)
12 *box* a small receptacle
     marmalade any kind of fruit preserve; commonly made with plums, dates, and quinces
13 *chops* mouth. The word usually referred to the outside of the mouth, so not only saliva-
     tion but drooling is probably implied.
14 *clap up* arrange hastily
14–15 *in hugger-mugger* secretly

BERGETTO

I will beget a race of wise men and constables, that shall cart whores
at their own charges, and break the Duke's peace ere I have done
myself. Come away!   *Exeunt*

[Act III, Scene ii]

Enter FLORIO, GIOVANNI, SORANZO, ANNABELLA,
PUTANA, *and* VASQUES

FLORIO

My lord Soranzo, though I must confess
The proffers that are made me have been great
In marriage of my daughter, yet the hope
Of your still-rising honours have prevailed
Above all other jointures. Here she is;   5
She knows my mind. Speak for yourself to her;
And hear you, daughter, see you use him nobly.
For any private speech I'll give you time;
Come, son, and you the rest, let them alone,
Agree as they may.

SORANZO   I thank you, sir.   10

GIOVANNI

[*Aside to* ANNABELLA] Sister, be not all woman: think on
me.

21 *constables* local officers of justice. Bergetto takes literally the usually ironic proverb
    (Tilley, C. 616) that they were especially intelligent. Since his name as Ford originally
    found it was spelt Bargetto (see Introduction), it may be relevant that the Italian
    equivalent of a constable was called a *bargello* (defined in *World* as 'a captain of
    sergeants').

21–22 *car . . . charges* administer justice to prostitutes at their own expense (rather than hav-
    ing it paid for out of the public purse; a sign of a rich man's public-spirited munificence).
    Public exhibition in a cart drawn through the streets was a common punishment for
    whores.

4 *have* has (governed by 'hope', not 'honours')

5 *jointures* gifts of property made to a woman by her fiancé as part of the marriage con-
    tract (here, offered by prospective fiancés)

9–10 *let . . . may* leave them alone in order that they may agree

11 *all woman* i.e. inconstant; women were proverbially subject to irrational change,
    particularly in sexual matters

SORANZO

  Vasques!

VASQUES

  My lord?

SORANZO

  Attend me without.

                       Exeunt all but SORANZO *and* ANNABELLA

ANNABELLA

  Sir, what's your will with me?   15

SORANZO

  Do you not know what I should tell you?

ANNABELLA   Yes,

  You'll say you love me.

SORANZO   And I'll swear it, too;

  Will you believe it?

ANNABELLA   'Tis not point of faith.

                 Enter GIOVANNI *above*

SORANZO

  Have you not will to love?

ANNABELLA   Not you.

SORANZO   Whom then?

ANNABELLA

  That's as the Fates infer.

GIOVANNI   [*Aside*] Of those I'm regent now.   20

SORANZO

  What mean you, sweet?

ANNABELLA   To live and die a maid.

SORANZO

  O, that's unfit.

GIOVANNI

  [*Aside*] Here's one can say that's but a woman's note.

14 *without* outside

16 *should* may be about to

16–18 lineation ed. (Doe . . . you? / Yes . . . mee. / And . . . it? / 'Tis . . . faith Q)

  18 *point of faith* a doctrine or article of belief essential for salvation; Annabella is saying, 'I don't have to believe it'.

  20 *infer* cause to happen

  20 *regent* ruler

  23 *but . . . note* only a woman's song, not the truth (in that Annabella is no longer a virgin); contrast Giovanni's next aside.

SORANZO
    Did you but see my heart, then would you swear –
ANNABELLA
    That you were dead.
GIOVANNI   [*Aside*] That's true, or somewhat near it.   25
SORANZO
    See you these true love's tears?
ANNABELLA   No.
GIOVANNI   [*Aside*] Now she winks.
SORANZO
    They plead to you for grace.
ANNABELLA   Yet nothing speak.
SORANZO
    O grant my suit!
ANNABELLA   What is't?
SORANZO   To let me live –
ANNABELLA
    Take it.
SORANZO   – Still yours.
ANNABELLA   That is not mine to give.
GIOVANNI
    [*Aside*] One such another word would kill his hopes.   30
SORANZO
    Mistress, to leave those fruitless strifes of wit,
    I know I have loved you long, and loved you truly;
    Not hope of what you have, but what you are
    Have drawn me on; then let me not in vain
    Still feel the rigour of your chaste disdain.   35
    I'm sick, and sick to th' heart.
ANNABELLA   Help, aqua-vitae!
SORANZO
    What mean you?
ANNABELLA   Why, I thought you had been sick!

---

26   *winks* closes her eyes (so that she cannot see tears which would otherwise be in plain
    sight). Since the whole exchange sardonically deflates Soranzo's conventional romantic
    metaphors by literalizing them (e.g. seeing his heart), this line may be ironic rather than
    an indication that Soranzo really is weeping.
31   *strifes of wit* banter (implying an aggressive edge)
36   *sick . . . heart* (a) mortally ill; (b) love-sick
    aqua-vitae distilled alcoholic liquor, taken medicinally

SORANZO
Do you mock my love?
GIOVANNI   [*Aside*] There, sir, she was too nimble.
SORANZO
[*Aside*] 'Tis plain, she laughs at me! [*To* ANNABELLA]
These scornful taunts
Neither become your modesty, or years.   40
ANNABELLA
You are no looking-glass, or, if you were,
I'd dress my language by you.
GIOVANNI   [*Aside*] I'm confirmed.
ANNABELLA
To put you out of doubt, my lord, methinks
Your common sense should make you understand
That if I loved you, or desired your love,   45
Some way I should have given you better taste;
But since you are a nobleman, and one
I would not wish should spend his youth in hopes,
Let me advise you here to forbear your suit,
And think I wish you well I tell you this.   50
SORANZO
Is't you speak this?
ANNABELLA   Yes, I myself. Yet know –
Thus far I give you comfort – if mine eyes
Could have picked out a man amongst all those
That sued to me, to make a husband of,
You should have been that man. Let this suffice.   55
Be noble in your secrecy, and wise.
GIOVANNI
[*Aside*] Why, now I see she loves me.
ANNABELLA   One word more:
As ever virtue lived within your mind,
As ever noble courses were your guide
As ever you would have me know you loved me,   60

---

38 *nimble* quick-witted
39–50 lineation ed. (prose in Q)
42 *dress . . . by you* order . . . according to your example. The phrase plays on the image of
     dressing one's hair at a mirror.
46 *given . . . taste* been nicer to you
50 *I . . . this* since I tell you this

Let not my father know hereof by you.
If I hereafter find that I must marry,
It shall be you or none.
SORANZO   I take that promise.
ANNABELLA
    O, O my head!
SORANZO   What's the matter, not well?
ANNABELLA
    O, I begin to sicken!
GIOVANNI   [*Aside*] Heaven forbid!   *Exit from above*   65
SORANZO
    Help, help, within there, ho!
    Look to your daughter, Signor Florio.

                Enter FLORIO, GIOVANNI, PUTANA

FLORIO
    Hold her up, she swoons.
GIOVANNI
    Sister, how d'ee?
ANNABELLA   Sick, brother, are you there?
FLORIO
    Convey her to her bed instantly, whilst I send for a physician –   70
    quickly I say!
PUTANA
    Alas, poor child!
                Exeunt [FLORIO, ANNABELLA, GIOVANNI, PUTANA];
                                    SORANZO *remains*

                    Enter VASQUES

VASQUES
    My lord.
SORANZO
    O Vasques, now I doubly am undone.
    Both in my present and my future hopes: 75
    She plainly told me that she could not love,
    And thereupon soon sickened, and I fear
    Her life's in danger.

---

66   s.p. *SORANZO* ed. (attributed to Giovanni in Q)

VASQUES

    [*Aside*] By'r Lady sir, and so is yours, if you knew all.
    [*Aloud*] 'Las, sir, I am sorry for that. Maybe 'tis but the   80
    maid's sickness, an overflux of youth – and then, sir, there is no
    such present remedy as present marriage. But hath she given you
    an absolute denial?

SORANZO

    She hath and she hath not. I'm full of grief,
    But what she said I'll tell thee as we go.   *Exeunt*   85

[Act III, Scene iii]

Enter GIOVANNI *and* PUTANA

PUTANA

    O sir, we are all undone, quite undone, utterly undone, and shamed
    forever! Your sister, O your sister!

GIOVANNI

    What of her? For heaven's sake speak, how does she?

PUTANA

    O that ever I was born to see this day!

GIOVANNI

    She is not dead, ha, is she?   5

PUTANA

    Dead! No, she is quick; 'tis worse, she is with child. You know what
    you have done, Heaven forgive 'ee! 'Tis too late to repent, now
    Heaven help us!

GIOVANNI

    With child? How dost thou know't?

---

81 *youth* a pubescent readiness for sex; the condition could be dangerous in excess
    ('overflux')

82 *present* immediate

1–2 prose ed. (Oh ... vndone, / And ... sister Q)

6 *quick* alive (but also implying 'quick with child', pregnant)

6–8 prose ed. (Dead? ... childe, / You ... 'ee, / 'Tis ... vs Q)

7–8 *'Tis ... us* There is an element of comic confusion in Putana's panic: in orthodox theol-
    ogy, heaven would help people only if they did repent.

PUTANA

How do I know't? Am I at these years ignorant what the   10
meanings of qualms and water-pangs be, of changing of colours,
queasiness of stomachs, pukings, and another thing that
I could name? Do not, for her and your credit's sake, spend
the time in asking how and which way 'tis so; she is quick,
upon my word. If you let a physician see her water you're   15
undone.

GIOVANNI

But in what case is she?

PUTANA

Prettily amended: 'twas but a fit, which I soon espied, and she must
look for often henceforward.

GIOVANNI

Commend me to her; bid her take no care,   20
Let not the doctor visit her, I charge you;
Make some excuse till I return. O me,
I have a world of business in my head!
Do not discomfort her.
How do this news perplex me! If my father   25
Come to her, tell him she's recovered well,
Say 'twas but some ill diet. D'ee hear, woman?
Look you to't.

PUTANA

I will, sir.   *Exeunt*

---

10 *at these years* at my age
11–12 *qualms . . . pukings* symptoms of pregnancy, including suddenly feeling faint ('qualms'),
        frequent need to urinate ('water-pangs'), and nausea ('morning sickness')
12 *another thing* Probably Annabella has stopped menstruating.
13 *credit's* reputation's
15 *water* urine. Examination of a patient's water was a usual method of medical diagnosis
        in the seventeenth century.
17 *case* condition, state
18 *amended* recovered, feeling better
        espied realized
20 *take no care* not to worry
23 *business* things to do
24–6 lineation ed. (Doe . . . mee! / If . . . well, Q)
25 *do* does (colloquial usage)

[Act III, Scene iv]

Enter FLORIO *and* RICHARDETTO [*disguised as the Doctor*]

FLORIO
And how d'ee find her, sir?
RICHARDETTO   Indifferent well:
I see no danger, scarce perceive she's sick,
But that she told me she had lately eaten
Melons, and as she thought, those disagreed
With her young stomach.
FLORIO   Did you give her aught?   5
RICHARDETTO
An easy surfeit-water, nothing else.
You need not doubt her health; I rather think
Her sickness is a fullness of her blood –
You understand me?
FLORIO   I do – you counsel well –
And once within these few days will so order't   10
She shall be married, ere she know the time.
RICHARDETTO
Yet let not haste, sir, make unworthy choice:
That were dishonour.
FLORIO   Master Doctor, no,
I will not do so neither. In plain words,
My lord Soranzo is the man I mean.   15

1 *Indifferent* Moderately
3–5 Melons must be eaten at the correct stage of ripeness; when over-ripe, they are likely to cause gastric ailments. The supposed cause of Annabella's illness corresponds with Richardetto's erroneous diagnosis (line 8).
6 *easy surfeit-water* mild indigestion remedy
8 *fullness of her blood* sexual ripeness (compare III.ii.81 and note). This was believed to be an ailment of female virgins; the usual remedy was for the young woman to have sex as soon as possible. It is ambiguous whether Richardetto, who is only posing as a physician, makes an honestly mistaken diagnosis; it is possible that he recognizes the signs of pregnancy but conceals them in order to inveigle Soranzo into a humiliating marriage to an unchaste woman.
10 *once* at some point
11 *ere . . . time* before she reaches the crucial point of her illness (i.e. the stage when continued abstinence from sex will be dangerous); there is probably a latent secondary meaning, unintended by Florio, referring to pregnancy ('the time' being the period of confinement before giving birth)

RICHARDETTO
A noble and a virtuous gentleman.

FLORIO
As any is in Parma. Not far hence
Dwells Father Bonaventure, a grave friar,
Once tutor to my son; now at his cell
I'll have 'em married.

RICHARDETTO   You have plotted wisely.   20

FLORIO
I'll send one straight to speak with him tonight.

RICHARDETTO
Soranzo's wise, he will delay no time.

FLORIO
It shall be so.

Enter FRIAR *and* GIOVANNI

FRIAR   Good peace be here and love!

FLORIO
Welcome, religious friar, you are one
That still bring blessing to the place you come to.   25

GIOVANNI
Sir, with what speed I could, I did my best
To draw this holy man from forth his cell
To visit my sick sister, that with words
Of ghostly comfort in this time of need
He might absolve her, whether she live or die.   30

FLORIO
'Twas well done, Giovanni: thou herein
Hast showed a Christian's care, a brother's love.
[*To the* FRIAR] Come, father, I'll conduct you to her chamber,
And one thing would entreat you.

FRIAR   Say on, sir.

---

21 lineation ed. (I'le ... straight / To ... to night Q)
23 Richardetto plays no part in the rest of the scene. It is possible that he exits here without witnessing the Friar's arrival; thus in the next scene he unwittingly gives Grimaldi wrong information about the marriage arrangements.
25 *still* always
29 *ghostly* spiritual

FLORIO

    I have a father's dear impression,   35

    And wish, before I fall into my grave,

    That I might see her married, as 'tis fit.

    A word from you, grave man, will win her more

    Than all our best persuasions.

FRIAR   Gentle sir,

    All this I'll say, that Heaven may prosper her.   *Exeunt* 40

[Act III, Scene v]

Enter GRIMALDI

GRIMALDI

    Now if the Doctor keep his word, Soranzo,

    Twenty to one you miss your bride. I know

    'Tis an unnoble act, and not becomes

    A soldier's valour; but in terms of love,

    Where merit cannot sway, policy must.   5

    I am resolved: if this physician

    Play not on both hands, then Soranzo falls.

    Enter RICHARDETTO [*disguised as the Doctor, with a box*]

RICHARDETTO

    You are come as I could wish. This very night

    Soranzo, 'tis ordained, must be affied

    To Annabella, and for aught I know,   10

    Married.

35 *a father's dear impression* This may mean a loving notion typical of fathers; or Florio may instead be saying that he bears the reproduced image ('impression') of his own father, and wants Annabella married so that she can 'print off' further 'impressions' by producing grandchildren (which is all the more important to him in view of the anxieties about Giovanni's health which he expresses at I.iii.5–8).

4 *terms of* matters relating to

5 *policy* devious cunning. The word had strongly negative connotations, which add emphasis to Grimaldi's point that all's fair in love.

7 *Play . . . on both hands* Act duplicitously

8–11 *You . . . Married* lineation ed. (prose in Q)

9 *affied* betrothed. A betrothal was the final stage before the formal solemnization of marriage, and was a legally binding contract.

GRIMALDI How!

RICHARDETTO   Yet your patience:
The place, 'tis Friar Bonaventure's cell.
Now I would wish you to bestow this night
In watching thereabouts. 'Tis but a night.
If you miss now! Tomorrow I'll know all.   15

GRIMALDI
Have you the poison?

RICHARDETTO   Here 'tis in this box.
Doubt nothing, this will do't; in any case,
As you respect your life, be quick and sure.

GRIMALDI
I'll speed him.

RICHARDETTO   Do. Away, for 'tis not safe
You should be seen much here. Ever my love.   20

GRIMALDI
And mine to you.   *Exit*

RICHARDETTO
So, if this hit, I'll laugh and hug revenge,
And they that now dream of a wedding-feast
May chance to mourn the lusty bridegroom's ruin.
But to my other business: 25
[*Calls*] Niece Philotis!

Enter PHILOTIS

PHILOTIS   Uncle?

RICHARDETTO   My lovely niece,
You have bethought 'ee?

PHILOTIS   Yes, and, as you counselled,
Fashioned my heart to love him; but he swears
He will tonight be married, for he fears
His uncle else, if he should know the drift,   30
Will hinder all, and call his coz to shrift.

---

12 *Friar* ed. (Fryars Q)
13 *bestow* spend
15 *If . . . now* You should act at once: there will never be a better opportunity
19 *speed him* kill him (literally, see him off on his journey)
22 *hit* succeed, 'come off'
    hug revenge i.e. having achieved it
25–7 lineation ed. (But . . . *Philotis*. / Vnkle. /My . . . bethought 'ee. /Yes . . . counsel'd Q)
31 *call... shrift* make him repent ('his coz' = Donado's kinsman, i.e. Bergetto)

RICHARDETTO

Tonight? Why, best of all. But let me see,
I – ha – yes, – so it shall be: in disguise
We'll early to the Friar's, I have thought on't.

Enter BERGETTO *and* POGGIO

PHILOTIS

Uncle, he comes.

RICHARDETTO   Welcome, my worthy coz.   35

BERGETTO

Lass, pretty lass; come buss, lass. [*Kisses her*] Aha, Poggio!

PHILOTIS

There's hope of this yet.

RICHARDETTO

You shall have time enough. Withdraw a little:
We must confer at large.

BERGETTO

[*To* PHILOTIS] Have you not sweetmeats, or dainty devices   40
for me?

PHILOTIS

You shall enough, sweetheart.

BERGETTO

Sweetheart! Mark that, Poggio. By my troth, I cannot choose
but kiss thee once more for that word 'sweetheart'. [*Kisses her*]

---

33   *I – ha – yes, – so* Richardetto mutters to himself as he turns things over in his mind. Most
       editors since Dodsley have interpreted Q's 'I' as signifying 'Ay' rather than the personal
       pronoun, and have modernized accordingly; both are conceivable, but one cannot ration-
       ally decide between the two when the dialogue is calculatedly incoherent; I have
       accordingly opted to retain the Q reading. In performance, the two words sound the
       same anyway.

36   *buss* kiss

37   s.p. *PHILOTIS* Q. This is Philotis' crucial line. Her previous remarks on the subject of her
       relationship with Bergetto (lines 27–8) suggest that she has accepted her impending mar-
       riage primarily in deference to Richardetto; now she speaks on her own account after
       having enjoyed the kiss. As an expression of emergent sexual feeling, it is matched by
       Bergetto's response to their next kiss (see note on line 45 below); the effect is to human-
       ize the relationship in preparation for the events of III.vii and IV.ii. Nonetheless, many
       previous editors have followed the nineteenth-century tradition of reassigning the line
       to either Richardetto (Gifford) or Poggio (Schmitz).

38–9 *Withdraw . . . at large* By 'at large', Richardetto may mean either 'at length' or 'as a group';
       either way, Bergetto will need to give his full attention, so he must 'withdraw' (stop kiss-
       ing Philotis).

[109]

Poggio, I have a monstrous swelling about my stomach,   45
whatsoever the matter be.

POGGIO

You shall have physic for't, sir.

RICHARDETTO

Time runs apace.

BERGETTO

Time's a blockhead! [*Kisses her*]

RICHARDETTO

Be ruled: when we have done what's fit to do,   50
Then you may kiss your fill, and bed her too.   *Exeunt*

[Act III, Scene vi]

Enter the FRIAR *in his study, sitting in a chair,*
ANNABELLA *kneeling and whispering to him,*
a table before them and wax-lights; she weeps, and
wrings her hands.

FRIAR

I am glad to see this penance, for, believe me,
You have unripped a soul so foul and guilty
As, I must tell you true, I marvel how
The earth hath borne you up. But weep, weep on:

45 *a monstrous swelling* Bergetto is becoming sexually excited ('stomach' here means his abdomen).

0 s.d. In the original production, the 'study' would again have been set in the discovery space (see note to II.ii.0 s.d.) and the traverse curtain drawn to show the characters already in position. (There is no other way literally to '*Enter . . . sitting' and 'kneeling'.*) The statement that this is the Friar's study (i.e. in his cell) seems to be contradicted by the reference in line 45 to Soranzo's waiting 'below', which suggests that the action takes place in Annabella's room at home, where Florio escorted the Friar in III.iv. (Barker suggests that, alternatively, 'in his study' may not be an indication of location at all, and may instead refer to 'the way the Friar is observed wrapped up in his contemplation of damnation'.) If the intended location is indeed Florio's house, then this is especially significant in that the scene's events obviate the original plan for Soranzo and Annabella to go to the Friar's cell (see note to line 42).
wax-lights candles or tapers

2 *unripped* disclosed

These tears may do you good. Weep faster yet,   5
Whiles I do read a lecture.
ANNABELLA   Wretched creature!
FRIAR
Ay, you are wretched, miserably wretched,
Almost condemned alive. There is a place –
List, daughter! – in a black and hollow vault,
Where day is never seen. There shines no sun,   10
But flaming horror of consuming fires,
A lightless sulphur, choked with smoky fogs
Of an infected darkness. In this place
Dwell many thousand thousand sundry sorts
Of never-dying deaths: there damnèd souls   15
Roar without pity; there are gluttons fed
With toads and adders; there is burning oil
Poured down the drunkard's throat, the usurer
Is forced to sup whole draughts of molten gold;
There is the murderer forever stabbed,   20
Yet can he never die; there lies the wanton
On racks of burning steel, whiles in his soul
He feels the torment of his raging lust.
ANNABELLA
Mercy, O mercy!
FRIAR   There stands these wretched things
Who have dreamt out whole years in lawless sheets   25

---

6   *Whiles* Whilst
    read a lecture deliver an admonitory speech
8–23   These lines are imitated from a passage in Thomas Nashe's *Pierce Penniless* (1592), where
       hell is described as 'a place of horror, stench, and darkness, where men see meat, but can
       get none, or are ever thirsty and ready to swelt for drink, yet have not the power to taste
       the cool streams that run at their feet; where . . . he that was a great drunkard here on
       earth hath his penance assigned him to carouse himself drunk with dishwash and vine-
       gar, and surfeit four times a day with sour ale and small beer; as so of the rest, the usurer
       to swallow molten gold, the glutton to eat nothing but toads, and the murderer to be
       still stabbed with daggers, but never die'. (Nashe, *Works*, ed. McKerrow, i. 218) Ford had
       previously imitated this passage in *Christ's Bloody Sweat* (1613).
9   *List* Listen
13   *infected* contaminated
25   *dreamt . . . years* Refers to a long period of moral insensibility (the incestuous liaison
     having the same relation to reality as does a dream).
     lawless sheets Metonymic for an unlawful sexual relationship.

And secret incests, cursing one another.
Then you will wish each kiss your brother gave
Had been a dagger's point; then you shall hear
How he will cry, 'O, would my wicked sister
Had first been damned, when she did yield to lust!'   30
But soft, methinks I see repentance work
New motions in your heart. Say, how is't with you?

ANNABELLA
Is there no way left to redeem my miseries?

FRIAR
There is: despair not. Heaven is merciful,
And offers grace even now. 'Tis thus agreed: 35
First, for your honour's safety, that you marry
The Lord Soranzo; next, to save your soul,
Leave off this life, and henceforth live to him.

ANNABELLA
Ay me!

FRIAR   Sigh not. I know the baits of sin
Are hard to leave. O, 'tis a death to do't.   40
Remember what must come! Are you content?

ANNABELLA
I am.

FRIAR I like it well; we'll take the time.
Who's near us there?

Enter FLORIO, GIOVANNI

FLORIO
Did you call, father?

FRIAR
Is Lord Soranzo come?

---

32 *motions* mental impulses
36–7 *First . . . next* Probably referring to simple chronological sequence rather than implying
    an order of priority.
38 *live to him* live as a faithful wife to Soranzo
40 *'tis . . . do't* it is intensely difficult and painful to tear oneself away from a sinful lifestyle
    (leading on to the implication that this metaphorical death is trivial compared with the
    absolute spiritual death suffered by those who fail to do so)
41 *what must come* Implying hell, if she does not carry through her repentance to the end.
42 *the time* the immediate opportunity (to have Soranzo and Annabella affianced). This
    supersedes the original betrothal plans which Florio mentioned to Richardetto in III.iv.,
    and Richardetto to Grimaldi in III.v.

FLORIO   He stays below.   45
FRIAR
  Have you acquainted him at full?
FLORIO   I have,
  And he is overjoyed.
FRIAR   And so are we.
  Bid him come near.
GIOVANNI   [*Aside*] My sister weeping, ha!
  I fear this friar's falsehood. [*Aloud*] I will call him.   *Exit*
FLORIO
  Daughter, are you resolved?
ANNABELLA   Father, I am.   50

       Enter GIOVANNI, SORANZO, *and* VASQUES

FLORIO
  My lord Soranzo, here
  Give me your hand; for that I give you this.
       [*He joins* SORANZO'S *and* ANNABELLA'S *hands*]
SORANZO
  Lady, say you so too?
ANNABELLA   I do, and vow
  To live with you and yours.
FRIAR   Timely resolved:
  My blessing rest on both! More to be done,   55
  You may perform it on the morning sun.   *Exeunt*

[Act III, Scene vii]

      Enter GRIMALDI *with his rapier drawn,*
        and a dark lantern

GRIMALDI
  'Tis early night as yet, and yet too soon

---

45 *stays below* waits downstairs
46–9 lineation ed. (Haue ... full? /1 ... ouer-ioy'd. / And ... neere. /My ... falshood, / I ... him Q)
52 s.d. The joining of hands (known in the period as 'handfasting') formally signifies the couple's betrothal.
53–4 *I do ... yours* lineation ed. (one line in Q)

0 s.d. *a dark lantern* a sealed lantern with a slide or shutter enabling a beam of light to be shown or hidden at will; it enabled a person (usually a criminal) to move about at night without attracting attention.

To finish such a work. Here I will lie
To listen who comes next.   *He lies down*

> *Enter* BERGETTO *and* PHILOTIS *disguised, and after*
> RICHARDETTO [*disguised as the Doctor*] *and* POGGIO

BERGETTO

We are almost at the place, I hope, sweetheart.

GRIMALDI

[*Aside*] I hear them near, and heard one say 'sweetheart':   5
'Tis he. Now guide my hand, some angry Justice,
Home to his bosom. [*Aloud*] Now have at you, sir!

> *Strikes* BERGETTO *and exit*

BERGETTO

O help, help, here's a stitch fallen in my guts! O for a flesh-tailor
quickly! Poggio!

PHILOTIS

What ails my love?   10

BERGETTO

I am sure I cannot piss forward and backward, and yet I am wet
before and behind. Lights, lights, ho lights!

PHILOTIS

Alas, some villain here has slain my love!

RICHARDETTO

O, Heaven forbid it! Raise up the next neighbours instantly,
Poggio, and bring lights.   *Exit* POGGIO   15
How is't, Bergetto? Slain? It cannot be; are you sure you're
hurt?

BERGETTO

O, my belly seethes like a porridge-pot. Some cold water, I shall
boil over else! My whole body is in a sweat, that you may wring
my shirt – feel here. Why, Poggio!   20

---

3   s.d. *disguised* They are probably wearing masks.
     after following them
6   *justice* a god or other supernatural force of justice
7   s.d. *Strikes* Runs him through with the poisoned rapier
8   *a stitch fallen* The phrase was normally used of a burst seam in an article of clothing
     (hence Bergetto's periphrasis for a surgeon, 'a flesh-tailor').
8–9 Prose ed. (Oh ... gutts, /Oh ... *Poggio* Q)
14–17 prose ed. (Oh ... neighbours / Instantly ... lights, / How ... slaine? / It ... hurt? Q)
20   s.d. *halberds* long-handled weapons combining an axe-blade and spear-head, carried by
     officers of the watch (who policed the city at night)

Enter POGGIO *with* OFFICERS, *and lights and halberds*

POGGIO
Here. Alas, how do you?

RICHARDETTO
Give me a light. What's here? All blood! O, sirs,
Signor Donado's nephew now is slain!
Follow the murderer with all the haste
Up to the city, he cannot be far hence.   25
Follow, I beseech you.

OFFICERS   Follow, follow, follow!
                                           Exeunt OFFICERS

RICHARDETTO
[*To* PHILOTIS] Tear off thy linen, coz, to stop his wounds.
[*To* BERGETTO] Be of good comfort, man.

BERGETTO
Is all this mine own blood? Nay then, goodnight with me.
Poggio, commend me to my uncle, dost hear? Bid him for   30
my sake make much of this wench. O, I am going the
wrong way sure, my belly aches so! O, farewell, Poggio
– O – O –   *Dies*

PHILOTIS
O, he is dead!

POGGIO   How! Dead?

RICHARDETTO   He's dead indeed.
'Tis now too late to weep. Let's have him home,   35
And with what speed we may find out the murderer.

POGGIO
O my master, my master, my master!   *Exeunt*

[Act III, Scene viii]

Enter VASQUES *and* HIPPOLITA

HIPPOLITA
Betrothed?

VASQUES
I saw it.

25 *the city* Parma's central administrative district
27 *linen* petticoats (usable as makeshift bandages)
31 *make much of* treat generously

HIPPOLITA
And when's the marriage-day?
VASQUES   Some two days hence.
HIPPOLITA
Two days? Why man, I would but wish two hours
To send him to his last and lasting sleep;   5
And Vasques, thou shalt see, I'll do it bravely.
VASQUES
I do not doubt your wisdom, nor, I trust, you my secrecy: I am
infinitely yours.
HIPPOLITA
I will be thine in spite of my disgrace.
So soon? O wicked man, I durst be sworn   10
He'd laugh to see me weep.
VASQUES
And that's a villainous fault in him.
HIPPOLITA
No, let him laugh: I'm armed in my resolves.
Be thou still true.
VASQUES
I should get little by treachery against so hopeful a preferment as 15
I am like to climb to.
HIPPOLITA
Even to my bosom, Vasques: let my youth
Revel in these new pleasures. If we thrive,
He now hath but a pair of days to live.   *Exeunt*

---

5 *his last . . . sleep* death
7–8 prose ed. (I . . . secresie, /I . . . yours Q)
9 *disgrace* This may refer either to the disgrace that will follow her open involvement in a
plot against Soranzo, or the disgrace that comes from a woman of her rank marrying a
servant.
15 *against* compared with
15 *preferment* promotion
17–18 *my youth . . . new pleasures* This could refer either to Soranzo and his marriage to
Annabella or to herself and her forthcoming liaison with Vasques.

[Act III, Scene ix]

Enter FLORIO, DONADO [*weeping*], RICHARDETTO
[*disguised as the Doctor*], POGGIO, *and* OFFICERS

FLORIO

    'Tis bootless now to show yourself a child,

    Signor Donado: what is done, is done.

    Spend not the time in tears, but seek for justice.

RICHARDETTO

    I must confess, somewhat I was in fault,

    That had not first acquainted you what love,   5

    Passed 'twixt him and my niece; but as I live,

    His fortune grieves me as it were mine own.

DONADO

    Alas, poor creature, he meant no man harm,

    That I am sure of.

FLORIO   I believe that too;

    But stay, my masters, are you sure you saw   10

    The murderer pass here?

OFFICER

    An it please you sir, we are sure we saw a ruffian with a naked

    weapon in his hand all bloody, get into my lord Cardinal's grace's

    gate: that we are sure of, but for fear of his grace – bless us! – we

    durst go no further.   15

DONADO

    Know you what manner of man he was?

OFFICER

    Yes, sure I know the man, they say a is a soldier. [*To* FLORIO]

    He that loved your daughter, sir, an't please ye, 'twas he for

    certain.

FLORIO

    Grimaldi, on my life!

OFFICER   Ay, ay, the same.   20

RICHARDETTO

    The Cardinal is noble: he no doubt

    Will give true justice.

---

1 *bootless* useless, pointless

DONADO
    Knock, someone, at the gate.
POGGIO
    I'll knock, sir.   POGGIO *knocks*
SERVANT (*Within*)
    What would 'ee?   25
FLORIO
    We require speech with the lord Cardinal
    About some present business. Pray inform
    His grace that we are here.

                Enter CARDINAL *and* GRIMALDI

CARDINAL
    Why, how now, friends! What saucy mates are you
    That know nor duty nor civility?   30
    Are we a person fit to be your host?
    Or is our house become your common inn,
    To beat our doors at pleasure? What such haste
    Is yours, as that it cannot wait fit times?
    Are you the masters of this commonwealth,   35
    And know no more discretion? O, your news
    Is here before you: you have lost a nephew,
    Donado, last night by Grimaldi slain.
    Is that your business? Well sir, we have knowledge on't:
    Let that suffice.
GRIMALDI [*Kneeling*] In presence of your grace,   40
    In thought I never meant Bergetto harm;
    But, Florio, you can tell with how much scorn
    Soranzo, backed with his confederates,
    Hath often wronged me. I to be revenged,

----

27 *present* urgent
29 *mates* an insulting epithet, implying low social status in those addressed
30 *nor . . . nor* neither . . . nor
34 *fit times* It is still night-time.
35 *the masters of this commonwealth* Not the political rulers but the municipal authorities
    responsible for policing the community.
39 *on't* of it
40 *In . . . grace* an affirmation of truthfulness, often used to strengthen a solemn oath
41 *In thought* In the conception of the crime. This was not an admissible defence in Eng-
    lish law.

For that I could not win him else to fight,　　　　　　　　45
Had thought by way of ambush to have killed him,
But was unluckily therein mistook,
Else he had felt what late Bergetto did.
And though my fault to him were merely chance,
Yet humbly I submit me to your grace,　　　　　　　　50
To do with me as you please.

CARDINAL　　　　　　　　Rise up, Grimaldi.

　　　　　　　　　　　　　　　[GRIMALDI *rises*]

You citizens of Parma, if you seek
For justice, know, as Nuncio from the Pope,
For this offence I here receive Grimaldi
Into his Holiness' protection.　　　　　　　　55
He is no common man, but nobly born
Of princes' blood, though you, sir Florio,
Thought him too mean a husband for your daughter.
If more you seek for, you must go to Rome,
For he shall thither. Learn more wit, for shame.　　　60
Bury your dead. Away, Grimaldi; leave 'em.

　　　　　　　　Exeunt CARDINAL *and* GRIMALDI

DONADO
Is this a churchman's voice? Dwells Justice here?

FLORIO
Justice is fled to heaven and comes no nearer.
Soranzo, was't for him? O impudence!
Had he the face to speak it, and not blush?　　　　　65
Come, come, Donado, there's no help in this
When cardinals think murder's not amiss.
Great men may do their wills, we must obey,
But Heaven will judge them for't another day.　　　*Exeunt*

45　*else* by any other means
49　*him* Bergetto
58　*mean* lowly
60　*wit* common sense
63　In classical mythology, Astraea, the goddess of justice, left the earth at the start of the iron age, driven away by human murderousness, and was placed in the heavens as the constellation of Virgo. The idea, best known from Ovid, *Metamorphoses* 1. 150, became a Renaissance commonplace, which the Cardinal's behaviour is taken to illustrate.

Act IV [Scene i]

A banquet. Hautboys. Enter the FRIAR, GIOVANNI,
ANNABELLA, PHILOTIS, SORANZO, DONADO, FLORIO,
RICHARDETTO [*disguised as the Doctor*], PUTANA, *and*
VASQUES

FRIAR

These holy rites performed, now take your times
To spend the remnant of the day in feast.
Such fit repasts are pleasing to the saints
Who are your guests, though not with mortal eyes
To be beheld. Long prosper in this day,   5
You happy couple, to each other's joy!

SORANZO

Father, your prayer is heard. The hand of goodness
Hath been a shield for me against my death,
And, more to bless me, hath enriched my life
With this most precious jewel, such a prize,   10
As earth hath not another like to this.
Cheer up, my love; and gentlemen, my friends,
Rejoice with me in mirth. This day we'll crown
With lusty cups to Annabella's health.

GIOVANNI

[*Aside*] O, torture! Were the marriage yet undone,   15
Ere I'd endure this sight, to see my love
Clipped by another, I would dare confusion
And stand the horror of ten thousand deaths.

VASQUES

Are you not well, sir?

---

 0 s.d. *Hautboys* Wind instruments with a shrill, reedy sound, usually played in a consort;
    the ancestor of the modern oboe.
 3–5 *the saints . . . beheld* The invisible presence of the saints (which might include angels and
    the blessed dead in heaven as well as canonized persons) is invoked as a sign of divine
    favour towards the marriage.
 5 *in this day* as a result of the marriage
 7 *The hand of goodness* God's providential action (to which he attributes the failure of
    Grimaldi's murder plot).
10 *this . . . jewel* Annabella
17 *Clipped* Embraced
    confusion destruction
19 *wait* see to your duties as an attendant

GIOVANNI   Prithee fellow, wait,
  I need not thy officious diligence.   20

FLORIO
  Signor Donado, come: you must forget
  Your late mishaps, and drown your cares in wine.

SORANZO
  Vasques!

VASQUES My lord?

SORANZO   Reach me that weighty bowl.
  Here, brother Giovanni, here's to you:
  Your turn comes next, though now a bachelor.   25
  Here's to your sister's happiness and mine!
              [SORANZO *drinks, and offers* GIOVANNI *the goblet*]

GIOVANNI
  I cannot drink.

SORANZO   What?

GIOVANNI   'Twill indeed offend me.

ANNABELLA
  Pray, do not urge him if he be not willing.
                                    [*Sounds are heard off-stage*]

FLORIO
  How now, what noise is this?

VASQUES
  O, sir, I had forgot to tell you: certain young maidens of Parma,   30
  in honour to Madam Annabella's marriage, have sent their loves
  to her in a masque, for which they humbly crave your patience
  and silence.

SORANZO
  We are much bound to them, so much the more
  As it comes unexpected. Guide them in.   35

23 *bowl* goblet
27 *offend* cause physical unease (*OED* 7), rather than offence in the modern sense; Giovanni
     is attempting to refuse politely.
32 *masque* an entertainment at an aristocratic wedding (or other formal occasion) involv-
     ing dancing by masked performers; in Ford's time (though not in the play), masques
     also incorporated elaborate dramatic narrative and spectacular scenery.
34–5 lineation ed. (prose in Q)
  35 s.d. *garlands of willow* associated with forsaken women (hence appropriate to Hippolita's
     view of her own situation)
     dance ed. (the word is repeated at the right-hand margin in Q)

[121]

Hautboys. Enter HIPPOLITA *and Ladies in [masks and]*
white robes, with garlands of willow.
Music and a dance.

SORANZO

Thanks, lovely virgins. Now might we but know
To whom we have been beholding for this love,
We shall acknowledge it.

HIPPOLITA   Yes, you shall know:
[*Unmasks*] What think you now?

ALL   Hippolita!

HIPPOLITA   'Tis she,
Be not amazed; nor blush, young lovely bride: 40
I come not to defraud you of your man.
[*To* SORANZO] 'Tis now no time to reckon up the talk
What Parma long hath rumoured of us both.
Let rash report run on: the breath that vents it
Will, like a bubble, break itself at last.   45
[*To* ANNABELLA] But now to you, sweet creature: lend's
    your hand.
Perhaps it hath been said that I would claim
Some interest in Soranzo, now your lord.
What I have right to do, his soul knows best;
But in my duty to your noble worth,   50
Sweet Annabella, and my care of you,
Here take Soranzo; take this hand from me.
I'll once more join what by the holy Church
Is finished and allowed. Have I done well?

SORANZO

You have too much engaged us.

HIPPOLITA   One thing more: 55
That you may know my single charity,

37 *love* act of kindness
44 *report* gossip
46 *lend's* lend us (= me)
48 *lord* husband
54 *allowed* approved
55 *engaged us* put us in your debt
56 *single* sincere (also implying celibate)
      charity disinterested love for one's fellow human beings (broader than the modern sense
      of the word). Charity was named as the principal Christian virtue in the 1568 and King
      James translations of 1 Corinthians 13.

Freely I here remit all interest
I e'er could claim, and give you back your vows;
And to confirm't – [*To* VASQUES] reach me a cup of wine–
My lord Soranzo, in this draught I drink   60
Long rest t'ee! [*Aside to* VASQUES] Look to it, Vasques.

VASQUES   [*Aside to* HIPPOLITA] Fear nothing.
                    He gives her a poisoned cup; she drinks

SORANZO
Hippolita, I thank you, and will pledge
This happy union as another life. Wine there!

VASQUES
You shall have none, neither shall you pledge her.

HIPPOLITA
How!   65

VASQUES
Know now, mistress she-devil, your own mischievous treachery
hath killed you. I must not marry you.

HIPPOLITA
Villain!

ALL
What's the matter?

VASQUES
Foolish woman, thou art now like a firebrand, that hath   70
kindled others and burnt thyself. *Troppo sperare inganna,* thy
vain hope hath deceived thee: thou art but dead. If thou hast
any grace, pray.

HIPPOLITA
Monster!

---

57 *remit* renounce
62 *pledge* drink from the same cup as a mark of respect
63 lineation ed. (This . . . life, / Wine there Q)
    union the union between him and Annabella which Hippolita has effected by joining
    their hands
66–7 prose ed. (Know . . . treachery / Hath . . . you Q)
70–1 *like . . . thyself* Imitated from *First Fruits* (I2ʳ): 'He is like a brand of fire, kindleth others
    and burneth himself.'
71 *Troppo . . . inganna* 'To hope too much deceives' (Italian). The idea was proverbial (Tilley,
    H. 608); Ford took the Italian version from *First Fruits* (I1ᵛ).
    inganna ed. (*niganna* Q)
72 *but dead* as good as dead
73 *grace* the divine power which enables a person to overcome original sin and act virtu-
    ously

VASQUES

Die in charity, for shame! [*To the others*] This thing of malice, this   75
woman, had privately corrupted me with promise of marriage,
under this politic reconciliation to poison my lord, whiles she
might laugh at his confusion on his marriage-day. I promised her
fair, but I knew what my reward should have been, and would will-
ingly have spared her life but that I was acquainted with the danger   80
of her disposition, and now have fitted her a just payment in her
own coin. There she is, she hath yet — [*To* HIPPOLITA] —and end
thy days in peace, vile woman. As for life, there's no hope: think
not on't.

ALL

Wonderful justice!   85

RICHARDETTO

Heaven, thou art righteous.

HIPPOLITA   O, 'tis true,
I feel my minute coming. Had that slave
Kept promise – O, my torment! – thou this hour
Hadst died, Soranzo. – Heat above hell-fire! –
Yet ere I pass away – cruel, cruel flames! –   90
Take here my curse amongst you: may thy bed
Of marriage be a rack unto thy heart. –
Burn, blood, and boil in vengeance! O my heart,
My flame's intolerable! – May'st thou live

---

75   *Die . . . shame* Die speaking well of others, rather than ill. Vasques makes ironic reference back to Hippolita's mendaciously claiming charity at line 56; (lineation ed.; printed
on a separate line in Q).

76   *marriage* ed. (malice Q)

77   *politic* cunningly deceitful

79   *I knew . . . been* She would have broken her promise and let Vasques be executed for the
murder.

79–81   *would . . . disposition* She is too vicious by nature to be allowed to live.

82   *yet . . . and end* ed. (yet —— and end Q) The two long dashes probably indicate illegi-
ble words in the copy. Roper suggests that the original text may have read something like
'she hath yet a minute to live. [*To* HIPPOLITA] Repent, and end thy days in peace'; this
might usefully be adopted in production.

87   *minute* the moment of death

89   *Heat* The perceived symptoms of poisoning in this period included an intense burning
sensation throughout the body; Ford portrayed the same effects at the end of his later
tragedy, *Love's Sacrifice* (1632), when Fernando is poisoned.

94   *My flame's intolerable* She imagines herself turning to flame, causing intolerable
pain.

To father bastards, may her womb bring forth   95
Monsters, and die together in your sins,
Hated, scorned and unpitied! – O – O!   *Dies*

FLORIO
Was e'er so vile a creature?
RICHARDETTO   Here's the end
Of lust and pride.
ANNABELLA   It is a fearful sight.
SORANZO
Vasques, I know thee now a trusty servant,   100
And never will forget thee. Come, my love,
We'll home, and thank the heavens for this escape.
Father and friends, we must break up this mirth:
It is too sad a feast.
DONADO   Bear hence the body.
FRIAR
[*Aside to* GIOVANNI] Here's an ominous change.   105
Mark this, my Giovanni, and take heed!
I fear the event: that marriage seldom's good,
Where the bride-banquet so begins in blood.
                    Exeunt [*with the body*]

[Act IV, Scene ii]

Enter RICHARDETTO *and* PHILOTIS

RICHARDETTO
My wretched wife, more wretched in her shame
Than in her wrongs to me, hath paid too soon

---

96 *Monsters* Deformed children (then considered ominous rather than unfortunate).
105 *change* i.e. from rejoicing to death
107 *event* subsequent outcome
108 *bride-banquet* wedding breakfast
    s.d. Vasques is the only servant present on stage (the text provides for no other atten-
    dants), so it is probably he who carries off Hippolita's body in an ironic visual conclusion
    to their duplicitous marital agreement. Single-handedly moving a 'corpse' is a cumber-
    some process which would give the actors of Richardetto and Philotis a moment to
    prepare for their immediate re-entry at the start of the next scene.

The forfeit of her modesty and life;
And I am sure, my niece, though vengeance hover,
Keeping aloof yet from Soranzo's fall,   5
Yet he will fall, and sink with his own weight.
I need not – now my heart persuades me so –
To further his confusion: there is one
Above begins to work; for, as I hear,
Debates already 'twixt his wife and him   10
Thicken and run to head. She, as 'tis said,
Slightens his love, and he abandons hers:
Much talk I hear. Since things go thus, my niece,
In tender love and pity of your youth,
My counsel is that you should free your years   15
From hazard of these woes by flying hence
To fair Cremona, there to vow your soul
In holiness a holy votaress.
Leave me to see the end of these extremes.
All human worldly courses are uneven: 20
No life is blessèd but the way to heaven.

PHILOTIS

Uncle, shall I resolve to be a nun?

RICHARDETTO

Ay, gentle niece, and in your hourly prayers
Remember me, your poor unhappy uncle.
Hie to Cremona now, as fortune leads,   25
Your home your cloister, your best friends your beads.

---

   3 *life* the promiscuous life she led
   8 *further his confusion* act to advance his destruction
 8–9 *one Above* God
  10 *Debates* Quarrels, disputes
  11 *run to head* develop towards a point of crisis, 'like a ripe boil ready to burst' (Morris)
  12 *Slightens* Disvalues, contemptuously rejects
  16 *flying* fleeing
  17 *Cremona* a city about 30 miles north of Parma, part of the state of Milan; it was notable for its many nunneries.
  18 *votaress* nun
  19 *extremes* desperate events
  20 *uneven* morally irregular
  25 *Hie* Go swiftly
  26 *beads* rosary beads, used by Roman Catholics to count prayers

Your chaste and single life shall crown your birth:
Who dies a virgin lives a saint on earth.

PHILOTIS

Then farewell world, and worldly thoughts adieu!
Welcome, chaste vows, myself I yield to you.   *Exeunt*   30

[Act IV, Scene iii]

Enter SORANZO, *unbraced* [*with his sword drawn*],
and ANNABELLA *dragged in*

SORANZO

Come, strumpet, famous whore! Were every drop
Of blood that runs in thy adulterous veins
A life, this sword – dost see't? – should in one blow
Confound them all. Harlot, rare, notable harlot,
That with thy brazen face maintain'st thy sin,   5
Was there no man in Parma to be bawd
To your loose, cunning whoredom else but I?
Must your hot itch and pleurisy of lust,
The heyday of your luxury, be fed
Up to a surfeit, and could none but I   10
Be picked out to be cloak to your close tricks,
Your belly-sports? Now I must be the dad

28 *lives* ed. (liue Q)
30 *yield* A young woman would also 'yield' in giving up her virginity (compare II.i.4), so
    the use of the word in this context gives Philotis' situation additional Poignancy.

0   s.d. *unbraced* with his clothes unfastened; not fully dressed
1   *famous* i.e. infamous
4   *Confound* Destroy
5   *maintain'st* either (*a*) persist in or (*b*) defend
6   *bawd* brothel-keeper, pimp; Soranzo pays for his wife's upkeep as a pimp supports a pros-
    titute, both for other men's sexual use.
7   *else but* other than
8–10 *Must . . . surfeit* Are you so incapable of controlling your sexual appetite
8   *pleurisy* (*a*) a feverish disease, alluding metaphorically to the heat of lust; (*b*) excess
9   *heyday . . . luxury* the highest pitch of lecherous excitement (referring, presumably, to
    the female orgasm)
11 *cloak* cover, disguise
    close secret

To all that gallimaufry that's stuffed
In thy corrupted bastard-bearing womb?
Why must I?

ANNABELLA   Beastly man, why, 'tis thy fate: 15
I sued not to thee, for – but that I thought
Your over-loving lordship would have run
Mad on denial – had ye lent me time
I would have told 'ee in what case I was;
But you would needs be doing.

SORANZO   Whore of whores!   20
Darest thou tell me this?

ANNABELLA   O yes, why not?
You were deceived in me: 'twas not for love
I chose you, but for honour. Yet know this:
Would you be patient yet and hide your shame,
I'd see whether I could love you.

SORANZO   Excellent quean!   25
Why, art thou not with child?

ANNABELLA   What needs all this,
When 'tis superfluous? I confess I am.

SORANZO
Tell me by whom.

ANNABELLA   Soft, sir, 'twas not in my bargain;
Yet somewhat, sir, to stay your longing stomach
I'm content t' acquaint you with. The man,   30
The more than man that got this sprightly boy –
For 'tis a boy, that's for your glory, sir,
Your heir shall be a son –

SORANZO   Damnable monster!

---

13 *gallimaufry* a hodge-podge of different materials; here used as a metaphor for a bastard
18 *on denial* at her refusal to marry him
19 *case* condition
20 *would ... doing* couldn't wait
24 *patient* stoical
25 *quean* sexually promiscuous woman
28 *'twas ... bargain* I didn't agree to tell you *that*
29 *somewhat* something
    stay ... stomach The primary sense is 'satisfy your hungry appetite (for information)', but 'longing' was also used of cravings in pregnancy, creating an ironic twist: Annabella has just been found to be pregnant, but it is Soranzo who has the unusual appetitive craving.
32 *that's ... glory* ed. (that for glory Q)

ANNABELLA
  Nay, an you will not hear, I'll speak no more.
SORANZO
  Yes, speak, and speak thy last.
ANNABELLA   A match, a match: 35
  This noble creature was in every part
  So angel-like, so glorious, that a woman
  Who had not been but human as was I,
  Would have kneeled to him, and have begged for love.
  You – why you are not worthy once to name   40
  His name without true worship, or indeed,
  Unless you kneeled, to hear another name him.
SORANZO
  What was he called?
ANNABELLA   We are not come to that.
  Let it suffice that you shall have the glory
  To father what so brave a father got.   45
  In brief, had not this chance fall'n out as't doth,
  I never had been troubled with a thought
  That you had been a creature; but for marriage,
  I scarce dream yet of that.
SORANZO
  Tell me his name!
ANNABELLA   Alas, alas, there's all.   50
  Will you believe?
SORANZO   What?
ANNABELLA   You shall never know.
SORANZO
  How!
ANNABELLA Never: if you do, let me be cursed.
SORANZO
  Not know it, strumpet! I'll rip up thy heart
  And find it there.

35 *A match, a match* It's a deal
37–9 *a woman . . . love* Annabella was only human, but even a woman who was above that
    frailty would have been overpowered by his beauty.
42 *another* someone else
45 *To father* To bear the name and play the part of a father in all except the biological sense
    brave excellent
48 *been a creature* existed
    but for marriage were it not for the fact that I am married to you

ANNABELLA   Do, do.

SORANZO   And with my teeth
Tear the prodigious lecher joint by joint.   55

ANNABELLA
Ha, ha, ha, the man's merry.

SORANZO   Dost thou laugh?
Come, whore, tell me your lover, or by truth
I'll hew thy flesh to shreds! Who is't?

ANNABELLA (*Sings*)
Che morte più dolce che morire per amore?

SORANZO
Thus will I pull thy hair, and thus I'll drag   60
Thy lust-belepered body through the dust.
Yet tell his name.

ANNABELLA (*Sings*)
Morendo in grazia a lui, morirei senza dolore.

SORANZO
Dost thou triumph? The treasure of the earth
Shall not redeem thee. Were there kneeling kings   65
Did beg thy life, or angels did come down
To plead in tears, yet should not all prevail
Against my rage. Dost thou not tremble yet?

ANNABELLA
At what? To die? No, be a gallant hangman:

---

55 *prodigious* unnatural and monstrous
59 What death is sweeter than to die for love? (Italian) This and the next Italian line (63)
    are copied directly from consecutive sayings in the section of *First Fruits* devoted to
    'amorous talk' (D1ᵛ); there, both refer to a man's love for a woman.
    più ed. (*pluis* Q)
61 *lust-belepered* made leprous through lust
63 Dying in favour with him, I would die without pain. (Italian).
    a lui ed. (*Lei* Q) *Lei* is the feminine pronoun, whereas Annabella, of course, is speaking
    of a man (*lui*). There is no certain evidence about whether Ford understood Italian: he
    never, so far as is known, used an Italian vernacular source, and the language is repre-
    sented in his other plays only by two words of *The Fancies, Chaste and Noble* ('*Signor
    mio*', I.ii.35) and a passage of 'cod' Italian in *The Sun's Darling* (II.i.179–81), which might
    anyway have been written by his collaborator, Thomas Dekker. It is possible that he sim-
    ply copied *lei* directly from *First Fruits*, not realizing the error of gender.
    morirei ed. (*morire* Q uncorrected; *morirere* Q corrected)
64 *triumph* exult
69 *hangman* In killing a woman, unequal to him in strength, Soranzo will be like an execu-
    tioner, whose victims are unable to defend themselves; the insult turns on the fact that
    the job was considered the basest kind of honest work, far beneath an aristocrat's dignity.

I dare thee to the worst, strike, and strike home.   70
I leave revenge behind, and thou shall feel't.

SORANZO
Yet tell me ere thou diest, and tell me truly,
Knows thy old father this?

ANNABELLA   No, by my life.

SORANZO
Wilt thou confess, and I will spare thy life?

ANNABELLA
My life! I will not buy my life so dear.   75

SORANZO
I will not slack my vengeance.

Enter VASQUES

VASQUES   What d'ee mean, sir?

SORANZO
Forbear, Vasques: such a damnèd whore
Deserves no pity.

VASQUES   Now the gods forfend!
And would you be her executioner, and kill her in your
rage too? O, 'twere most unmanlike! She is your wife. What   80
faults hath been done by her before she married you, were not
against you. Alas poor lady, what hath she committed which
any lady in Italy in the like case would not? Sir, you must be
ruled by your reason and not by your fury: that were unhuman
and beastly.   85

SORANZO
She shall not live.

VASQUES
Come, she must. You would have her confess the authors of
her present misfortunes, I warrant 'ee. 'Tis an unconscionable
demand, and she should lose the estimation that I, for my
part, hold of her worth, if she had done it. Why sir, you ought not 90
of all men living to know it. Good sir, be reconciled. Alas, good
gentlewoman!

71 *I . . . behind* there will be someone left alive to avenge my death (meaning the lover whose
    identity Soranzo does not know)
76 *slack* put off, delay
78 *forfend* forbid
87 *the authors of* those responsible for
88 *unconscionable* unreasonably excessive

ANNABELLA
    Pish, do not beg for me: I prize my life
    As nothing. If the man will needs be mad,
    Why, let him take it.
SORANZO   Vasques, hear'st thou this?   95
VASQUES
    Yes, and commend her for it: in this she shows the nobleness
    of a gallant spirit, and beshrew my heart but it becomes
    her rarely. [*Aside to* SORANZO] Sir, in any case smother your
    revenge: leave the scenting-out your wrongs to me. Be ruled,
    as you respect your honour, or you mar all. [*Aloud*] Sir, if   100
    ever my service were of any credit with you, be not so
    violent in your distractions. You are married now: what a
    triumph might the report of this give to other neglected
    suitors! 'Tis as manlike to bear extremities, as godlike to
    forgive.   105
SORANZO
    O Vasques, Vasques, in this piece of flesh,
    This faithless face of hers, had I laid up
    The treasure of my heart! [*To* ANNABELLA] Hadst thou
        been virtuous,
    Fair, wicked woman, not the matchless joys
    Of life itself had made me wish to live   110
    With any saint but thee. Deceitful creature,
    How hast thou mocked my hopes, and in the shame
    Of thy lewd womb even buried me alive!
    I did too dearly love thee.
VASQUES (*Aside* [*to* SORANZO]) This is well;
    Follow this temper with some passion, be brief and moving: 'tis   115
    for the purpose.

97   *beshrew* may evil befall
      but unless
100   *your honour* ed. (hour honour Q)
101   *credit with* value to
102   *distractions* deranged fits
102–5 *You . . . suitors* As a winner in the marriage game, Soranzo should not give losers the
      opportunity to gloat; contrast Florio's views at I.ii.55.
104   *bear extremities* put up with others' egregious behaviour
115–16 prose ed. (Follow . . . passion, / Bee . . . purpose Q)
115   *Follow . . . passion* Vasques tells Soranzo how to play it next: having toned down ('tem-
      pered') his rage against Annabella, he should now show her the strong emotion she
      provokes in him.

SORANZO

[*To* ANNABELLA] Be witness to my words thy soul and
    thoughts,
And tell me, didst not think that in my heart
I did too superstitiously adore thee?

ANNABELLA

I must confess, I know you loved me well.   120

SORANZO

And wouldst thou use me thus? O Annabella,
Be thou assured, whatsoe'er the villain was
That thus hath tempted thee to this disgrace,
Well he might lust, but never loved like me;
He doted on the picture that hung out   125
Upon thy cheeks, to please his humorous eye,
Not on the part I loved, which was thy heart,
And, as I thought, thy virtues.

ANNABELLA   O my lord!
These words wound deeper than your sword could do.

VASQUES

Let me not ever take comfort, but I begin to weep myself, so much   130
I pity him. Why, madam, I knew when his rage was overpassed
what it would come to.

SORANZO

Forgive me, Annabella. Though thy youth
Hath tempted thee above thy strength to folly,
Yet will not I forget what I should be,   135
And what I am, a husband: in that name
Is hid divinity. If I do find
That thou wilt yet be true, here I remit
All former faults, and take thee to my bosom.

---

117 Let your soul and thoughts be witness to my words
119 *did . . . thee* worshipped you like a pagan idol
122 *thou* ed. (thus Q)
126 *humorous* capricious
134 *above thy strength* beyond her power to resist
136–7 *a husband . . . divinity* An orthodox notion of the time, which drew biblical authority
from Ephesians 5. 22–3: 'Wives, submit yourselves unto your own husbands, as unto the
Lord. For the husband is the head of the wife, even as Christ is the head of the church'.
The point of the analogy here is that Soranzo will exercise the divine prerogative of for-
giveness if Annabella repents.
138 *remit* forgive, pardon

VASQUES

    By my troth, and that's a point of noble charity.   140

ANNABELLA [*Kneeling*]

    Sir, on my knees –

SORANZO   Rise up, you shall not kneel.

    Get you to your chamber; see you make no show

    Of alteration. I'll be with you straight.

    My reason tells me now that 'tis as common

    To err in frailty as to be a woman.   145

    Go to your chamber.   *Exit* ANNABELLA

VASQUES

    So, this was somewhat to the matter. What do you think of
    your heaven of happiness now, sir?

SORANZO

    I carry hell about me: all my blood

    Is fired in swift revenge.   150

VASQUES

    That may be, but know you how, or on whom? Alas, to
    marry a great woman, being made great in the stock to your
    hand, is a usual sport in these days; but to know what
    ferret it was that haunted your cunny-berry, there's the
    cunning.   155

SORANZO

    I'll make her tell herself, or –

VASQUES

    Or what? You must not do so. Let me yet persuade your sufferance
    a little while: go to her, use her mildly, win her, if it be possible,

---

142–3 *see . . . alteration* now that you are penitent, let there be no backsliding

144–5 Ford was probably recalling *Hamlet* I.ii.146: 'frailty, thy name is woman'.

  147 *to the matter* pertinent, relevant

  152 *great* pregnant

152–3 *great . . . hand* The phrase contains complex and significant word-play around the mul-
      tiple meanings of 'stock'. The primary sense is 'handed over to you already pregnant'
      ('stock' = body), with the latent, ironic suggestion that Soranzo has been spared the pro-
      creative drudgery of begetting an heir. A similar implication comes from 'stock' as (*a*) a
      handle (which is now the right size to fit Soranzo's hand) and (*b*) the stem of a plant
      into which a graft is inserted. The word could also mean 'rabbit-hole' (anticipating 'cunny-
      berry' later in the sentence).

  154 *ferret* ed. (*Secret* Q)

       cunny-berry (*a*) rabbit ('cony') burrow; (*b*) vagina ('cunny')

  155 *cunning* intelligent, artful skill

  157 *sufferance* toleration

to a voluntary, to a weeping tune. For the rest, if all hit, I will
not miss my mark. Pray sir, go in. The next news I tell you shall   160
be wonders.

SORANZO
Delay in vengeance gives a heavier blow.   *Exit*

VASQUES
Ah, sirrah, here's work for the nonce! I had a suspicion of
a bad matter in my head a pretty whiles ago; but after my
madam's scurvy looks here at home, her waspish perverseness   165
and loud fault-finding, then I remembered the proverb,
that where hens crow and cocks hold their peace there are sorry
houses. 'Sfoot, if the lower parts of a she-tailor's cunning can
cover such a swelling in the stomach, I'll never blame a false
stitch in a shoe whiles I live again. Up, and up so quick? And so   170
quickly too? 'Twere a fine policy to learn by whom; this must be
known.

Enter PUTANA [*weeping*]

And I have thought on't: here's the way, or none. [*To* PUTANA]
What, crying, old mistress? Alas, alas, I cannot blame 'ee. We have
a lord, Heaven help us, is so mad as the devil himself, the more   175
shame for him.

---

159   *voluntary* a spontaneous part of a musical performance, chosen by the performer rather
        than prescribed by the score; the musical equivalent of an ad lib (here applied to
        Annabella's penitence).
159   *if all hit* if everything comes off (perhaps with a latent pun on archery, developed in
        'mark')
160   *mark* target
163   *the nonce* the present occasion
167–8 *where . . . houses* domestic life is unsatisfactory when the wife dominates her husband
        (which was considered contrary to the natural order of things). The proverb (Tilley, H.
        778) is closely adapted from *First Fruits* (I1ᵛ).
168–9 *lower . . . stomach* A 'she-tailor' is probably a male tailor who makes clothing *for* women,
        rather than one who is a woman herself. His 'cunning', in the sense of 'skill', is metonymic
        for its product, i.e. the dress he makes; the 'lower parts' of that dress might be artfully
        designed to conceal ('cover') the outward signs of pregnancy. Vasques also puns on 'cun-
        ning' in its usual modern sense, with 'lower parts' implying baseness.
170   *Up . . . quickly* The passage works as a cascade of meaning from word to word: 'up' means
        pregnant (referring to the physical swelling of the stomach); 'quick' means both preg-
        nant and rapidly; and the latter sense is then picked up in 'quickly'.
172   s.d. ed. (after 'or none.' in Q)
175   *mad* angry

PUTANA

O Vasques, that ever I was born to see this day! Doth he use thee
so too sometimes, Vasques?

VASQUES

Me! Why, he makes a dog of me; but if some were of my
mind, I know what we would do. As sure as I am an honest   180
man, he will go near to kill my lady with unkindness. Say she be
with child, is that such a matter for a young woman of her years
to be blamed for?

PUTANA

Alas, good heart, it is against her will full sore.

VASQUES

I durst be sworn, all his madness is for that she will not confess   185
whose 'tis, which he will know, and when he doth know it, I am
so well acquainted with his humour that he will forget all straight.
Well, I could wish she would in plain terms tell all, for that's the
way indeed.

PUTANA

Do you think so?   190

VASQUES

Foh, I know't, provided that he did not win her to't by force. He
was once in a mind that you could tell, and meant to have wrung
it out of you, but I somewhat pacified him for that. Yet sure you
know a great deal.

PUTANA

Heaven forgive us all, I know a little, Vasques.   195

VASQUES

Why should you not? Who else should? Upon my conscience, she
loves you dearly, and you would not betray her to any affliction
for the world.

PUTANA

Not for all the world, by my faith and troth, Vasques.

VASQUES

'Twere pity of your life if you should; but in this you should both   200
relieve her present discomforts, pacify my lord, and gain yourself
everlasting love and preferment.

177–8 prose ed. (O ... day, / Doth ... *Vasques?*. Q)
    187 *humour* characteristic temperament
          that as to be able to say that
    191 *provided ... force* Everything will be alright so long as Soranzo finds out before resort-
          ing to violence; Putana is being given the opportunity to forestall such an eventuality.

PUTANA

Dost think so, Vasques?

VASQUES

Nay, I know't. Sure 'twas some near and entire friend.

PUTANA

'Twas a dear friend indeed; but – 205

VASQUES

But what? Fear not to name him: my life between you and danger.
Faith, I think 'twas no base fellow.

PUTANA

Thou wilt stand between me and harm?

VASQUES

Ud's pity, what else? You shall be rewarded too. Trust me.

PUTANA

'Twas even no worse than her own brother. 210

VASQUES

Her brother Giovanni, I warrant 'ee?

PUTANA

Even he, Vasques. As brave a gentleman as ever kissed fair lady. O,
they love most perpetually.

VASQUES

A brave gentleman indeed; why, therein I commend her
choice. [*Aside*] Better and better. [*To her*] You are sure 215
'twas he?

PUTANA

Sure; and you shall see he will not be long from her, too.

VASQUES

He were to blame if he would. But may I believe thee?

204 *entire* intimate
209 *Ud's pity* an oath, minced from 'God's pity'
   what else? of course!
211 *'ee*? Q. The punctuation could be modernized as a question mark or an exclamation
   mark (the two symbols were not differentiated in the early seventeenth century): the latter would signal shock at what Putana is saying, whereas the former would show a
   punctilious concern to make absolutely sure. Either version is possible, but as a question
   the line is more in keeping with the gentle way in which Vasques has drawn the information out of Putana so far.
218 *to blame* blameworthy

PUTANA

Believe me! Why, dost think I am a Turk or a Jew! No, Vasques, I have known their dealings too long to belie 220 them now.

VASQUES

Where are you? There within, sirs!

Enter BANDITTI

PUTANA

How now, what are these?

VASQUES

You shall know presently. Come sirs, take me this old damnable hag, gag her instantly, and put out her eyes. 225 Quickly, quickly!

[*The* BANDITTI *tie up* PUTANA]

PUTANA

Vasques, Vasques!

VASQUES

Gag her I say! 'Sfoot, d'ee suffer her to prate? What, d'ee fumble about? Let me come to her. I'll help your old gums, you toad-bellied bitch! [*He gags* PUTANA] Sirs, carry her closely into the 230 coal-house and put out her eyes instantly. If she roars, slit her nose. D'ee hear? Be speedy and sure.

Exeunt [BANDITTI] *with* PUTANA

Why, this is excellent and above expectation! Her own brother? O horrible! To what a height of liberty in damnation hath the devil trained our age! Her brother, well! There's yet but a 235 beginning. I must to my lord, and tutor him better in his

---

219   *a Turk or a Jew* Implying a person unworthy of belief, not to be trusted; in effect, Putana avers her story 'as I am a Christian' (Turks and Jews being the principal *non*-Christian races known to early seventeenth-century Europe).

222   s.d. *BANDITTI* Members of an organized gang of robbers such as operated in the mountains and forests of Italy

224   *presently* immediately

224–6   prose ed. (You . . . presently, / Come . . . *hagge,* / Gag . . . quickly Q)

229–30   *toad-bellied* a general term of opprobrium and abuse; compare Thomas Dekker, *The Noble Spanish Soldier* (1622), IV.ii.179: 'Sirrah, you sarsaparilla rascal toad-guts'.

234   *liberty* licentiousness

235   *trained* tempted, enticed

points of vengeance. Now I see how a smooth tale goes beyond a smooth tail.

Enter GIOVANNI

But soft, what thing comes next? Giovanni! As I would wish. My belief is strengthened: 'tis as firm as winter and   240
summer.

GIOVANNI
Where's my sister?

VASQUES
Troubled with a new sickness, my lord; she's somewhat ill.

GIOVANNI
Took too much of the flesh, I believe.

VASQUES
Troth sir, and you I think have e'en hit it; but my virtuous   245
lady –

GIOVANNI
Where's she?   [*Gives him money*]

VASQUES
In her chamber; please you visit her? She is alone. Your liberality hath doubly made me your servant, and ever shall, ever –   *Exit* GIOVANNI   250

Enter SORANZO

Sir, I am made a man. I have plied my cue with cunning and success. I beseech you, let's be private.

237–8 *how a smooth . . . tail* how a plausible lie overcomes a wanton woman (literally, a well-lubricated, easily penetrated vagina). Ford is probably recalling *The Duchess of Malfi*: 'What cannot a neat knave with a smooth tale / Make a woman believe?' (I.ii.258–9)

238 s.d. ed. (after 'next?' in Q)

240–1 *as firm . . . summer* as certain as the interchange of the seasons

244 *took . . . flesh* overindulged in (*a*) meat and (*b*) sex ('flesh' = penis); the latter sense is, of course, unintended by Giovanni, though heard by Vasques.

245 *hit it* correctly identified the reason

245–6 Prose ed. (Troth . . . it, / But . . . Lady Q)

249 *liberality* generosity in tipping

251 *made a man* a man who has been entirely successful (in seventeenth-century idiom, 'a made man'; a misprint is not impossible)

251–2 *plied . . . success* played my part effectively. The metaphor is of an actor giving cue-lines that prompt his fellow-performers to speak (here, to utter the incriminating information that Vasques wants to know).

SORANZO

My lady's brother's come; now he'll know all.

VASQUES

Let him know't: I have made some of them fast enough.
How have you dealt with my lady?   255

SORANZO

Gently, as thou hast counselled. O, my soul
Runs circular in sorrow for revenge!
But Vasques, thou shalt know –

VASQUES

Nay, I will know no more, for now comes your turn to
know. I would not talk so openly with you. Let my young   260
master take time enough, and go at pleasure: he is sold to
death, and the devil shall not ransom him. Sir, I beseech you, your
privacy.

SORANZO

No conquest can gain glory of my fear.   *Exeunt*

Act V [Scene i]

Enter ANNABELLA *above, [with a letter written in
blood]*

ANNABELLA

Pleasures farewell, and all ye thriftless minutes
Wherein false joys have spun a weary life;
To these my fortunes now I take my leave.

---

254 *fast* secure; referring to Putana, whom Vasques has just silenced and imprisoned
254–5 prose ed. (Let ... enough, / How ... Lady ? Q)
257 *Runs circular* Moves without getting anywhere (like an animal tied to a stake)
260 *know* be told
        openly publicly
264 No matter what success ('conquest') Vasques has achieved, it will be unable to overcome
        ('gain glory of') Soranzo's fear.
264 s.d. ed. (*Exit.* Q)

  1 *thriftless* (spiritually) unprofitable

Thou precious Time, that swiftly ridest in post
Over the world to finish up the race   5
Of my last fate, here stay thy restless course
And bear to ages that are yet unborn
A wretched, woeful woman's tragedy.
My conscience now stands up against my lust
With depositions charactered in guilt,   10

Enter FRIAR [*below*]

And tells me I am lost. Now I confess,
Beauty that clothes the outside of the face
Is cursèd if it be not clothed with grace.
Here like a turtle, mewed up in a cage
Unmated, I converse with air and walls,   15
And descant on my vile unhappiness.
O Giovanni, that hast had the spoil
Of thine own virtues and my modest fame,
Would thou hadst been less subject to those stars
That luckless reigned at my nativity!   20

4–8 Time's riding 'in post' refers partly to the speed with which events move towards the
      play's destructive climax. Some earlier tragic heroes, such as Marlowe's Doctor Faustus,
      wish for time to stop in order to avert their doom; Annabella, however, accepts its
      inevitability and simply wants Time, conceived as a 'post' (messenger), to stop and col-
      lect her story for delivery to future times.
9–10 Annabella imagines her conscience as her prosecutor in a trial, armed with depositions
      (formal written testimony, accepted as evidence in court in the absence of a witness);
      the ink with which these documents are written ('charactered') is her own moral guilt,
      so they substantiate the case against her in their medium as well as their content. Given
      the concern with unconventional writing media (also the blood with which Annabella
      has written her letter; and see note on 'gall' to V.iii.75), 'guilt' may also pun on 'gilt', sug-
      gesting gold lettering, 'as of words deserving display' (Roper).
10 *depositions* ed. (dispositions Q)
13 *grace* both moral virtue and the favour of God which enables it (compare note to IV.i.73)
14 *turtle* a turtle-dove, an emblem of wedded constancy in English folklore because it took
      only a single mate in its lifetime. Thus Annabella is 'unmated' in her captivity, even
      though her husband has access to her, because her original partner, Giovanni, does not.
      mewed up confined (sometimes in preparation for slaughter)
15 *Unmated* Without a mate
      converse with keep company with (but also implying 'have sex with', here suggesting
      enforced celibacy)
16 *descant on* discourse at large about
17 *had the spoil* (*a*) destroyed; (*b*) plundered

O, would the scourge due to my black offence
Might pass from thee, that I alone might feel
The torment of an uncontrolled flame!

FRIAR

[*Aside*] What's this I hear?

ANNABELLA   That man, that blessed friar,
Who joined in ceremonial knot my hand   25
To him whose wife I now am, told me oft
I trod the path to death, and showed me how.
But they who sleep in lethargies of lust
Hug their confusion, making Heaven unjust,
And so did I.

FRIAR   [*Aside*] Here's music to the soul!   30

ANNABELLA

Forgive me, my good genius, and this once
Be helpful to my ends: let some good man
Pass this way, to whose trust I may commit
This paper double-lined with tears and blood;
Which being granted, here I sadly vow   35
Repentance, and a leaving of that life
I long have died in.

FRIAR   Lady, Heaven hath heard you,
And hath by providence ordained that I
Should be his minister for your behoof.

ANNABELLA

Ha, what are you?   40

FRIAR   Your brother's friend the friar,
Glad in my soul that I have lived to hear

---

23   *an uncontrolled flame* the fire of hell
25   *ceremonial knot* bonds of matrimony
29   *making . . . unjust* supposing that divine law is unjust (because arbitrarily restrictive)
31   *genius* guardian angel; see note to II.ii.154.
32   *ends* purposes
34   *double-lined . . . blood* The paper is written ('lined', i.e. with lines of script) in her blood,
     but her penitent tears have also dropped onto the page, making it 'double-lined'.
35   *sadly* solemnly, seriously
37   *died* died spiritually
39   *behoof* benefit, advantage
42   *peace* quiet (here implying privacy)

This free confession 'twixt your peace and you.
What would you, or to whom? Fear not to speak.

ANNABELLA

Is Heaven so bountiful? Then I have found
More favour than I hoped. Here, holy man.   45

Throws [down the] letter

Commend me to my brother, give him that,
That letter; bid him read it and repent.
Tell him that I – imprisoned in my chamber,
Barred of all company, even of my guardian,
Who gives me cause of much suspect – have time   50
To blush at what hath passed. Bid him be wise,
And not believe the friendship of my lord.
I fear much more than I can speak. Good father,
The place is dangerous, and spies are busy:
I must break off. You'll do't?

FRIAR   Be sure I will,   55
And fly with speed. My blessing ever rest
With thee, my daughter. Live to die more blessed.   *Exit*

ANNABELLA

Thanks to the heavens, who have prolonged my breath
To this good use. Now I can welcome death.   *Exit*

[Act V, Scene ii]

Enter SORANZO *and* VASQUES

VASQUES

Am I to be believed now? First, marry a strumpet that cast herself
away upon you but to laugh at your horns? To feast on your dis-

---

49 *my guardian* Putana
50 *Who* The absence of whom
      suspect suspicion, anxiety
52 *not believe* mistrust

1 *Am . . . now?* prose ed. (printed on a separate line in Q)
2 *but* only
      horns Said to grow on cuckolds' foreheads.

grace, riot in your vexations, cuckold you in your bride-bed, waste
your estate upon panders and bawds?

SORANZO

No more, I say no more!   5

VASQUES

A cuckold is a goodly tame beast, my lord.

SORANZO

I am resolved; urge not another word.
My thoughts are great, and all as resolute
As thunder. In meantime I'll cause our lady
To deck herself in all her bridal robes,   10
Kiss her, and fold her gently in my arms.
Begone. Yet hear you, are the banditti ready
To wait in ambush?

VASQUES

Good sir, trouble not yourself about other business than
your own resolution: remember that time lost cannot be   15
recalled.

SORANZO

With all the cunning words thou canst, invite
The states of Parma to my birthday's feast.
Haste to my brother-rival and his father,
Entreat them gently, bid them not to fail.   20
Be speedy and return.

VASQUES

Let not your pity betray you till my coming back: think upon incest
and cuckoldry.

SORANZO

Revenge is all the ambition I aspire;
To that I'll climb or fall. My blood's on fire!   *Exeunt*   25

---

3   *riot in* revel in, derive disorderly pleasure from
8   *great* pregnant; the metaphor was commonly used of someone hatching a revenge plot
     (compare *Othello*, I.iii.395–6).
10   *deck* clothe
15–16 *time . . . recalled* Proverbial (Tilley, T. 332).
18   *states* senior government figures, dignitaries
22–3 prose ed. (Let . . . backe, / Thinke . . . *Cuckoldry* Q)
24   *aspire* wish for

[Act V, Scene iii]

Enter GIOVANNI

GIOVANNI
Busy opinion is an idle fool,
That, as a school-rod keeps a child in awe,
Frights the unexperienced temper of the mind.
So did it me, who, ere my precious sister
Was married, thought all taste of love would die   5
In such a contract; but I find no change
Of pleasure in this formal law of sports.
She is still one to me, and every kiss
As sweet and as delicious as the first
I reaped when yet the privilege of youth   10
Entitled her a virgin. O, the glory
Of two united hearts like hers and mine!
Let poring bookmen dream of other worlds:
My world and all of happiness is here,
And I'd not change it for the best to come.   15
A life of pleasure is Elysium.

Enter FRIAR

Father, you enter on the jubilee
Of my retired delights. Now I can tell you,
The hell you oft have prompted is nought else

1–3 Giovanni's point is that what common consensus ('opinion') teaches people to believe
and expect is contradicted by actual experience.
1 *Busy* Meddlesome, interfering
idle ineffectual
2 *school-rod* a bundle of birch-twigs used as an instrument of corporal punishment, but
more commonly displayed as a threat, 'For terror, not to use' (Shakespeare, *Measure for
Measure*, I.iii.26)
7 *in . . . sports* as a result of the legalization (by marriage) of Annabella's sexual activity
8 *one* the same as she was
10–11 *when . . . virgin* when she was still a virgin. The point is expressed in quasilegal terms,
with 'virgin' a title bestowed on Annabella ('entitled') by legal right or prerogative ('privilege').
13 *bookmen* scholars
17 *jubilee* time of celebration
18 *retired* private
19 *prompted* spoken of

But slavish and fond superstitious fear,   20
And I could prove it, too –
FRIAR   Thy blindness slays thee.
                                        Gives the letter
Look there, 'tis writ to thee.
GIOVANNI
From whom?
FRIAR
Unrip the seals and see.
                    [GIOVANNI *opens and reads the letter*]
The blood's yet seething hot, that will anon   25
Be frozen harder than congealèd coral.
Why d'ee change colour, son?
GIOVANNI   'Fore heaven, you make
Some petty devil factor 'twixt my love
And your religion-maskèd sorceries.
Where had you this?
FRIAR   Thy conscience, youth, is seared,   30
Else thou wouldst stoop to warning.
GIOVANNI   'Tis her hand,
I know't, and 'tis all written in her blood.
She writes I know not what. Death? I'll not fear
An armèd thunderbolt aimed at my heart.
She writes we are discovered. Pox on dreams   35
Of low faint-hearted cowardice! Discovered?
The devil we are! Which way is't possible?
Are we grown traitors to our own delights?

---

21 *I could prove it* The choice of words ('could' rather than 'can') is interesting, perhaps suggesting that he cannot be bothered.
25–6 These lines may be spoken as an aside while Giovanni reads.
26 *congealèd coral* ed. (congeal'd Corrall Q). Coral was thought to be an undersea plant which hardened when exposed to the air.
28 *factor* intermediary (in carrying the letter from Annabella, Giovanni's 'love'); Ford uses the word similarly in *The Broken Heart*, II.i.10.
30 *seared* cauterized (and so rendered insensible)
31 *stoop to warning* restrain your own impulses in heeding and obeying the warning you have been given
38 Giovanni assumes that he and Annabella are the only ones who know, forgetting Putana (and also the Friar)

Confusion take such dotage; 'tis but forged!
This is your peevish chattering, weak old man. 40

Enter VASQUES

Now, sir, what news bring you?

VASQUES
My lord, according to his yearly custom keeping this day a feast in
honour of his birthday, by me invites you thither. Your worthy
father, with the Pope's reverend Nuncio and other magnificoes of
Parma, have promised their presence. Will't please you to be of the 45
number?

GIOVANNI
Yes, tell them I dare come.

VASQUES
Dare come?

GIOVANNI
So I said; and tell him more, I will come.

VASQUES
These words are strange to me. 50

GIOVANNI
Say I will come.

VASQUES
You will not miss?

GIOVANNI
Yet more? I'll come! Sir, are you answered?

VASQUES
So I'll say. My service to you. *Exit*

FRIAR
You will not go, I trust.

GIOVANNI Not go! For what? 55

FRIAR
O do not go! This feast, I'll gage my life,
Is but a plot to train you to your ruin.
Be ruled, you sha' not go.

---

39 *dotage* nonsense (literally, senile ramblings)
40 s.d. ed. (after line 41 in Q)
52 *miss* fail to come
56 *gage* stake, wager
57 *train* allure, entice

GIOVANNI   Not go? Stood Death
  Threat'ning his armies of confounding plagues,
  With hosts of dangers hot as blazing stars,   60
  I would be there. Not go! Yes, and resolve
  To strike as deep in slaughter as they all,
  For I will go.
FRIAR   Go where thou wilt; I see
  The wildness of thy fate draws to an end,
  To a bad, fearful end. I must not stay   65
  To know thy fall: back to Bologna I
  With speed will haste, and shun this coming blow.
  Parma, farewell; would I had never known thee,
  Or aught of thine! Well, young man, since no prayer
  Can make thee safe, I leave thee to despair.   *Exit*   70
GIOVANNI
  Despair or tortures of a thousand hells,
  All's one to me: I have set up my rest.
  Now, now, work serious thoughts on baneful plots:
  Be all a man, my soul; let not the curse
  Of old prescription rend from me the gall   75
  Of courage, which enrols a glorious death.
  If I must totter like a well-grown oak,
  Some under-shrubs shall in my weighty fall
  Be crushed to splits; with me they all shall perish.   *Exit*

60 *blazing stars* comets, thought to be a portent of death
69 *aught of thine* i.e Giovanni
    young man ed. (*Youngman* Q)
71 s.p. GIOVANNI ed. (missing in Q)
72 *set . . . rest* committed myself to my final venture, staked my all. In tte card game primero,
    the 'rest' was a stake held in reserve; to 'set up' your rest was to make a final wager which,
    if lost, would put you out of the game.
73 *baneful* destructive
75 *prescription* prescribed social behaviour (such as not murdering people at parties)
    gall The primary sense is 'aggression', from the bodily fluid which supposedly induced
    this; but Giovanni imagines it in terms of an organ (the gall-bladder) being ripped out
    of his body. 'Gall' also referred to a secretion from the oak tree (compare line 77) that
    was used in making ink (hence the next line's suggestion of its 'enrolling' his death, writ-
    ing it down in the roll of honour).
79 *splits* splinters

[Act V, Scene iv]

Enter SORANZO, VASQUES *and* BANDITTI

SORANZO
You will not fail, or shrink in the attempt?

VASQUES
I will undertake for their parts. [*To the* BANDITTI] Be sure,
my masters, to be bloody enough, and as unmerciful as if you
were preying upon a rich booty on the very mountains of
Liguria. For your pardons, trust to my lord; but for reward you   5
shall trust none but your own pockets.

ALL THE BANDITTI
We'll make a murder.

SORANZO [*Giving them money*]
Here's gold, here's more; want nothing. What you do
Is noble and an act of brave revenge.
I'll make ye rich banditti, and all free.   10

ALL [THE BANDITTI]
Liberty! Liberty!

VASQUES
Hold, take every man a vizard. When ye are withdrawn,
keep as much silence as you can possibly. You know the
watchword, till which be spoken, move not; but when you
hear that, rush in like a stormy flood. I need not instruct ye in your   15
own profession.

ALL [THE BANDITTI]
No, no, no.

VASQUES
In, then. Your ends are profit and preferment. Away!

Exeunt BANDITTI

---

2 *undertake . . . parts* guarantee that they will play their parts efficiently
5 *Liguria* a mountainous region of north-western Italy between Parma and Genoa
5–10 *pardons . . . free* Banditti were thought often to be banished men (like the outlaws in *The
     Two Gentlemen of Verona*) who would welcome the opportunity to return to civil soci-
     ety as free men if a pardon were offered them.
8 *want* lack
8–9 lineation ed. (prose in Q)
12 *vizard* mask
18 *ends* purposes

SORANZO

The guests will all come, Vasques?

VASQUES

Yes, sir, and now let me a little edge your resolution. You see noth-   20
ing is unready to this great work but a great mind in you. Call to
your remembrance your disgraces, your loss of honour, Hippolita's
blood, and arm your courage in your own wrongs: so shall you
best right those wrongs in vengeance which you may truly call
your own.   25

SORANZO

'Tis well: the less I speak, the more I burn,
And blood shall quench that flame.

VASQUES

Now you begin to turn Italian! This beside, when my young
incest-monger comes, he will be sharp set on his old bit. Give
him time enough; let him have your chamber and bed at   30
liberty; let my hot hare have law ere he be hunted to his
death, that if it be possible he may post to hell in the very act of
his damnation.

Enter GIOVANNI

SORANZO

It shall be so; and see, as we would wish,
He comes himself first. [*To* GIOVANNI] Welcome, my
     much-loved brother.   35
Now I perceive you honour me; you're welcome.
But where's my father?

19   s.d. *Exeunt* ed. (*Exit* Q)
20   *Yes, sir* prose ed. (printed on a separate line in Q)
     edge sharpen (like a sword); compare II.ii.63.
28   *you . . . Italian* In becoming more vindictive, Soranzo is living up to his nationality:
     among the perceived national characteristics of the Italians was vengefulness.
29   *sharp . . . old bit* keen for sex with his former paramour
31   *hare* supposed to have an excessive sexual appetite
     law a head-start
32   *post* ride swiftly
32–3 *in . . . damnation* If killed while committing a mortal sin, without time to repent, Gio-
     vanni will go directly to hell.
37   *father* father-in-law (= Florio)

GIOVANNI   With the other states,
   Attending on the Nuncio of the Pope
   To wait upon him hither. How's my sister?
SORANZO
   Like a good housewife, scarcely ready yet;   40
   You're best walk to her chamber.
GIOVANNI   If you will.
SORANZO
   I must expect my honourable friends.
   Good brother, get her forth.
GIOVANNI   You are busy, sir.   *Exit*
VASQUES
   Even as the great devil himself would have it! Let him go and glut
   himself in his own destruction.   *Flourish*   45
   Hark, the Nuncio is at hand. Good sir, be ready to receive
   him.

        Enter CARDINAL, FLORIO, DONADO, RICHARDETTO
             [*disguised as the Doctor*] *and Attendants*

SORANZO [*To the* CARDINAL]
   Most reverend lord, this grace hath made me proud
   That you vouchsafe my house; I ever rest
   Your humble servant for this noble favour.   50
CARDINAL
   You are our friend, my lord. His Holiness
   Shall understand how zealously you honour
   Saint Peter's vicar in his substitute:
   Our special love to you.
SORANZO   Signors, to you
   My welcome, and my ever best of thanks   55

---

40 *good* typical – here meaning one who is idle and wastes time; a relevant secondary sense
    of 'housewife', in Soranzo's mouth though not in Giovanni's ears, is 'hussy', promiscu-
    ous woman.
42 *expect* await
45 s.d. *Flourish* A fanfare of trumpets played upon the arrival of an important personage
    (here, the Cardinal).
48 *this grace* the honour the Cardinal does Soranzo in visiting his feast
49 *vouchsafe* deign to visit
53 *Saint Peter's vicar* the Pope (St Peter was thought to be the first Pope; his successors were
    thus considered his 'vicars', substitute representatives)

[151]

For this so memorable courtesy.
Pleaseth your grace to walk near?
CARDINAL   My lord, we come
To celebrate your feast with civil mirth,
As ancient custom teacheth. We will go.
SORANZO
Attend his grace, there! Signors, keep your way.   60

Exeunt

[Act V, Scene v]

Enter GIOVANNI *and* ANNABELLA *lying on a bed*

GIOVANNI
What, changed so soon? Hath your new sprightly lord
Found out a trick in night-games more than we
Could know in our simplicity? Ha, is't so?
Or does the fit come on you to prove treacherous
To your past vows and oaths?
ANNABELLA   Why should you jest   5
At my calamity, without all sense
Of the approaching dangers you are in?
GIOVANNI
What danger's half so great as thy revolt?
Thou art a faithless sister, else thou know'st
Malice, or any treachery beside,   10
Would stoop to my bent brows. Why, I hold fate

---

60 *keep your way* carry on in the direction you're going

0 s.d. In the original production, the bed would probably have been pushed out onto the stage through the discovery space with Annabella (and perhaps Giovanni) already on it. In view of Soranzo's comment that she is 'scarcely ready yet' (V.iv.40), it is possible that Annabella is not yet fully dressed. If she is (as her reference to 'gay attires' at line 20 suggests), then she is wearing the 'bridal robes' which Soranzo mentioned earlier (V.ii.11).

1 *changed* Referring to her disposition, not her clothes.

1–3 *Hath . . . simplicity?* Giovanni wants to know if Soranzo's love-making is more exciting than his own.

4 *the fit* a capricious impulse

6 *calamity* distress

8 *revolt* disloyalty

11 *stoop . . . brows* submit on seeing me frown

Clasped in my fist, and could command the course
Of time's eternal motion hadst thou been
One thought more steady than an ebbing sea.
And what? You'll now be honest, that's resolved?   15

ANNABELLA

Brother, dear brother, know what I have been,
And know that now there's but a dining-time
'Twixt us and our confusion. Let's not waste
These precious hours in vain and useless speech.
Alas, these gay attires were not put on   20
But to some end; this sudden solemn feast
Was not ordained to riot in expense:
I that have now been chambered here alone,
Barred of my guardian, or of any else,
Am not for nothing at an instant freed   25
To fresh access. Be not deceived, my brother:
This banquet is an harbinger of death
To you and me; resolve yourself it is,
And be prepared to welcome it.

GIOVANNI   Well then,
The schoolmen teach that all this globe of earth   30
Shall be consumed to ashes in a minute.

ANNABELLA

So I have read too.

GIOVANNI   But 'twere somewhat strange
To see the waters burn. Could I believe
This might be true, I could believe as well
There might be hell or heaven.

---

18   *confusion* destruction
21   *solemn* (*a*) ceremonious; (*b*) lavish
22   *riot in expense* waste money
25–6 *freed . . . access* allowed visitors again after her imprisonment
30–3 The belief that the world would end in a conflagration of purging fire was as old as the
        Stoic philosophers of ancient Greece, but its principal biblical authority was Revelation
        21. 1: 'And I saw a new heaven and a new earth; for the first heaven and the first earth
        were passed away; and there was no more sea'; see also 2 Peter 3. 10. Scholastic philoso-
        phers (known as 'schoolmen') attempted to rationalize this notion: the classic statement
        is that of Thomas Aquinas in *Summa Theologica* 3. 74. Giovanni astutely locates one of
        the holes in the case which had previously puzzled St Augustine (*City of God* 20. 16):
        whereas the Stoics had taught that the seas would gradually dry up in the heat, the idea
        of a destruction that is instantaneous and absolute ('all this globe . . . consumed to ashes
        in a minute') entails believing that water will burn.

ANNABELLA   That's most certain.   35

GIOVANNI
A dream, a dream; else in this other world
We should know one another.

ANNABELLA   So we shall.

GIOVANNI
Have you heard so?

ANNABELLA   For certain.

GIOVANNI   But d'ee think
That I shall see you there, you look on me;
May we kiss one another, prate or laugh,   40
Or do as we do here?

ANNABELLA   I know not that,
But, good, for the present, what d'ee mean
To free yourself from danger? Some way think
How to escape. I'm sure the guests are come.

GIOVANNI
Look up, look here: what see you in my face?   45

ANNABELLA
Distraction and a troubled countenance.

GIOVANNI
Death, and a swift repining wrath. Yet look:
What see you in mine eyes?

ANNABELLA   Methinks you weep.

GIOVANNI
I do indeed: these are the funeral tears
Shed on your grave; these furrowed up my cheeks   50
When first I loved and knew not how to woo.
Fair Annabella, should I here repeat
The story of my life, we might lose time.
Be record all the spirits of the air,
And all things else that are, that day and night,   55

37–41   lineation ed. (Wee . . . another. / So . . . shall. / Haue . . . so? / For certaine. / But . . . thinke, /
       That . . . there, / You . . . mee. / May . . . another, / Prate . . . laugh, / Or . . . here? / I . . . that Q)
40   *prate* talk casually
42   *good* A vocative term of address (like the modern 'dear'), often used by Ford. *mean* intend
      to do
47   *repining* angrily discontented
54   *spirits of the air* In hermetic philosophy 'middle spirits', neither angels nor devils, whose
      bodies were made of air; they could hear human speech but not read thoughts.

Early and late, the tribute which my heart
Hath paid to Annabella's sacred love
Hath been these tears, which are her mourners now.
Never till now did Nature do her best
To show a matchless beauty to the world,   60
Which in an instant, ere it scarce was seen,
The jealous Destinies required again.
Pray, Annabella, pray. Since we must part,
Go thou white in thy soul to fill a throne
Of innocence and sanctity in heaven.   65
Pray, pray, my sister.
ANNABELLA   Then I see your drift.
Ye blessed angels, guard me!
GIOVANNI   So say I.
Kiss me. [*They kiss*] If ever after-times should hear
Of our fast-knit affections, though perhaps
The laws of conscience and of civil use   70
May justly blame us, yet when they but know
Our loves, that love will wipe away that rigour
Which would in other incests be abhorred.
Give me your hand. How sweetly life doth run
In these well-coloured veins! How constantly   75
These palms do promise health! But I could chide
With Nature for this cunning flattery.
Kiss me again. Forgive me.
ANNABELLA   With my heart.   [*They kiss*]
GIOVANNI
Farewell.
ANNABELLA Will you be gone?
GIOVANNI   Be dark, bright sun,
And make this midday night, that thy gilt rays   80
May not behold a deed will turn their splendour
More sooty than the poets feign their Styx!

62 *required again* demanded the return of (in death)
68 *after-times* future ages
70 *civil use* the customary practice of civilization
72 *rigour* passionate extremity
77 *cunning flattery* It is flattering in that the apparent healthiness of her hand belies her
    imminent fate (i.e. death).
82 *Styx* principal river of the classical underworld, with poisonous black waters

[155]

One other kiss, my sister.

ANNABELLA   What means this?

GIOVANNI

To save thy fame, and kill thee in a kiss.   *Stabs her*

Thus die, and die by me, and by my hand.   85

Revenge is mine; honour doth love command.

ANNABELLA

O brother, by your hand?

GIOVANNI   When thou art dead

I'll give my reasons for't; for to dispute

With thy (even in thy death) most lovely beauty,

Would make me stagger to perform this act   90

Which I most glory in.

ANNABELLA

Forgive him, Heaven – and me my sins. Farewell,

Brother, unkind, unkind. – Mercy, great Heaven!

– O – O!   *Dies*

GIOVANNI

She's dead. Alas, good soul. The hapless fruit   95

That in her womb received its life from me,

Hath had from me a cradle and a grave.

I must not dally. This sad marriage-bed,

In all her best, bore her alive and dead.

Soranzo, thou hast missed thy aim in this: 100

I have prevented now thy reaching plots

And killed a love, for whose each drop of blood

I would have pawned my heart. Fair Annabella,

How over-glorious art thou in thy wounds,

Triumphing over infamy and hate!   105

Shrink not, courageous hand; stand up, my heart,

And boldly act my last and greater part!

                        Exit with the body

---

84   *fame* reputation
90   *stagger* hesitate
93   *unkind* (*a*) cruel; (*b*) unnatural (literally, unlike the behaviour expected of a kinsman)
95   *hapless* unfortunate, luckless
101   *prevented* forestalled
      reaching subtle and cunning
104   *over-glorious* superlatively beautiful

[Act V, Scene vi]

A banquet [is set out]. Enter CARDINAL, FLORIO,
DONADO, SORANZO, RICHARDETTO [*disguised as the
Doctor*], VASQUES, *and Attendants; they take their
places [at the table]*

VASQUES

[*Aside to* SORANZO] Remember sir, what you have to do: be wise
and resolute.

SORANZO

[*Aside to* VASQUES] Enough, my heart is fixed. [*To* CARDINAL]
    Pleaseth your grace
To taste these coarse confections? Though the use
Of such set entertainments more consists   5
In custom than in cause, yet, reverend sir,
I am still made your servant by your presence.

CARDINAL

And we your friend.

SORANZO

But where's my brother Giovanni?

Enter GIOVANNI *with a heart upon his dagger*

GIOVANNI

Here, here, Soranzo, trimmed in reeking blood   10
That triumphs over death, proud in the spoil
Of love and vengeance! Fate, or all the powers
That guide the motions of immortal souls
Could not prevent me.

CARDINAL   What means this?

FLORIO

Son Giovanni!

SORANZO [*Aside*] Shall I be forestalled?   15

GIOVANNI

Be not amazed: if your misgiving hearts

---

0 s.d. *take their places* sit at the table
4–6 *the use . . . cause* formal entertainments like this are held more because of the inertia of
    custom than for any good reason
10 *trimmed* covered (literally, decorated)
    reeking steaming

Shrink at an idle sight, what bloodless fear
Of coward passion would have seized your senses,
Had you beheld the rape of life and beauty
Which I have acted? My sister, O my sister!   20
FLORIO
Ha! What of her?
GIOVANNI   The glory of my deed
Darkened the midday sun, made noon as night.
You came to feast, my lords, with dainty fare.
I came to feast too, but I digged for food
In a much richer mine than gold or stone   25
Of any value balanced. 'Tis a heart,
A heart, my lords, in which is mine entombed.
Look well upon't; d'ee know't?
VASQUES
What strange riddle's this?
GIOVANNI
'Tis Annabella's heart, 'tis. Why d'ee startle?   30
I vow 'tis hers: this dagger's point ploughed up
Her fruitful womb, and left to me the fame
Of a most glorious executioner.
FLORIO
Why, madman, art thyself?
GIOVANNI
Yes father, and, that times to come may know   35
How as my fate I honoured my revenge,
List, father: to your ears I will yield up
How much I have deserved to be your son.
FLORIO
What is't thou say'st?
GIOVANNI   Nine moons have had their changes,
Since I first throughly viewed and truly loved   40
Your daughter and my sister.
FLORIO   How! Alas,
My lords, he's a frantic madman!

17 *idle* mere
19 *rape* violent theft
25 *stone* precious stones, jewels
26 *balanced* calculated
40 *throughly* thoroughly
41–2 *How . . . madman* lineation ed. (one line in Q)

GIOVANNI   Father, no.
  For nine months' space in secret I enjoyed
  Sweet Annabella's sheets; nine months I lived
  A happy monarch of her heart and her.   45
  Soranzo, thou know'st this: thy paler cheek
  Bears the confounding print of thy disgrace,
  For her too fruitful womb too soon bewrayed
  The happy passage of our stol'n delights,
  And made her mother to a child unborn.   50
CARDINAL
  Incestuous villain!
FLORIO   O, his rage belies him!
GIOVANNI
  It does not, 'tis the oracle of truth:
  I vow it is so.
SORANZO   I shall burst with fury.
  Bring the strumpet forth!
VASQUES
  I shall, sir.   *Exit*
GIOVANNI   Do, sir. Have you all no faith   55
  To credit yet my triumphs? Here I swear
  By all that you call sacred, by the love
  I bore my Annabella whilst she lived,
  These hands have from her bosom ripped this heart.

                    Enter VASQUES

  Is't true or no, sir?
VASQUES   'Tis most strangely true.   60
FLORIO
  Cursèd man! Have I lived to –   *Dies*
CARDINAL   Hold up, Florio.

46   *paler cheek* It is not clear whether he means paler than his own (which is covered in blood) or Florio's (which may be blushing in shame at Giovanni's revelations).

48   *bewrayed* revealed

49   *passage* The word implies both a sequence of events and a mutual interchange of amorous experience between lovers; Ford was probably recalling Shakespeare's Prologue to *Romeo and Juliet* ('The fearful passage of their death-marked love').

51   *rage* frenzy

59   s.d. ed. (after line 60a in Q)

61   *Hold up, Florio* The words are ambiguous, their sense depending on whether the Cardinal already recognizes that Florio is dead. As here punctuated, the Cardinal offers encouragement to Florio in the belief that he is still alive; dramatic irony thus cuts against

[*To* GIOVANNI] Monster of children, see what thou hast
    done,
Broke thy old father's heart! Is none of you
Dares venture on him?

GIOVANNI   Let 'em! O, my father,
How well his death becomes him in his griefs!   65
Why, this was done with courage; now survives
None of our house but I, gilt in the blood
Of a fair sister and a hapless father.

SORANZO
Inhuman scorn of men, hast thou a thought
T' outlive thy murders?

GIOVANNI   Yes, I tell thee yes;   70
For in my fists I bear the twists of life.
Soranzo, see this heart which was thy wife's:
Thus I exchange it royally for thine,   [*Stabs him*]
And thus, and thus. Now brave revenge is mine.

VASQUES
I cannot hold any longer. You sir, are you grown insolent in your   75
butcheries? Have at you!

                [VASQUES *and* GIOVANNI] *fight*
GIOVANNI
Come, I am armed to meet thee.

---

    the Cardinal, making him yet another character wrong-footed by Giovanni's actions in
    this and the previous scene. Without the comma, the Cardinal would be ordering atten-
    dants to show Giovanni the dead body (hence 'see what thou hast done' in the next line).
67 *gilt* covered; but in performance, assonance may also convey the implication of blood-guilt
68 *hapless* unlucky, ill-fated
71 *twists* woven threads. Giovanni alludes to the thread representing a human life which
    was spun, woven, and cut by the Fates of classical mythology, whom he earlier claimed
    to rule (III.ii.20).
73 s.d. In order to be able to use his dagger on Soranzo, Giovanni must by this point have
    removed the heart from it; it was probably still on the dagger (or else held in his other
    hand) moments before when he referred to it as 'this heart' (72). The question of when
    to remove it and what to do with it is open to any number of inventive solutions in per-
    formance. (In the 1991–2 RSC production, for example, Giovanni physically placed the
    organ in Soranzo's hands before stabbing him, making the exchange of one heart for
    another a semi-literal one; in Griffi's film version he uses Soranzo's own dagger.) Alter-
    natively, Giovanni may have more than one weapon (e.g. rapier as well as dagger), and
    uses the other on Soranzo here.

VASQUES

   No, will it not be yet? If this will not, another shall. – Not yet? I
   shall fit you anon. – [*Calls off stage*] Vengeance!

       Enter BANDITTI [*all masked and armed*]

GIOVANNI

   Welcome! Come more of you, whate'er you be,   80
   I dare your worst. –
              [*The* BANDITTI *surround and wound him*]
   O, I can stand no longer; feeble arms,
   Have you so soon lost strength?

VASQUES

   Now you are welcome, sir! Away, my masters, all is done.
   Shift for yourselves; your reward is your own; shift for   85
   yourselves.

BANDITTI

   Away, away!   *Exeunt* BANDITTI

VASQUES

   How d'ee, my lord? See you this? How is't?

SORANZO

   Dead, but in death well pleased, that I have lived
   To see my wrongs revenged on that black devil.   90
   O Vasques, to thy bosom let me give
   My last of breath: let not that lecher live – O!   *Dies*

VASQUES

   The reward of peace and rest be with him, my ever dearest lord
   and master.

GIOVANNI

   Whose hand gave me this wound?   95

VASQUES

   Mine, sir, I was your first man. Have you enough?

---

78   *will . . . yet?* Giovanni is taking a long time to die.
79   *fit you* deal with you
     Vengeance The watchword to call in the banditti (see V.iv.13–14).
84–6 prose ed. (Now . . . Sir, / Away . . . done, / Shift . . . owne, / Shift . . . selues Q)
85–6 *Shift for yourselves* Every man for himself
91–2 *give . . . breath* i.e. in a dying instruction
93–4 prose ed. (The . . . him, / My . . . Maister Q)

GIOVANNI

    I thank thee: thou hast done for me
    But what I would have else done on myself.
    Art sure thy lord is dead?

VASQUES   O impudent slave,

    As sure as I am sure to see thee die.   100

CARDINAL

    Think on thy life and end, and call for mercy.

GIOVANNI

    Mercy? Why, I have found it in this justice.

CARDINAL

    Strive yet to cry to heaven.

GIOVANNI   O, I bleed fast.

    Death, thou art a guest long looked-for: I embrace
    Thee and thy wounds. O, my last minute comes.   105
    Where'er I go, let me enjoy this grace,
    Freely to view my Annabella's face.   *Dies*

DONADO

    Strange miracle of justice!

CARDINAL

    Raise up the city! We shall be murdered all!

VASQUES

    You need not fear, you shall not. This strange task being   110
    ended, I have paid the duty to the son which I have vowed to
    the father.

CARDINAL

    Speak, wretched villain, what incarnate fiend
    Hath led thee on to this?

VASQUES

    Honesty, and pity of my master's wrongs. For know, my   115
    lord, I am by birth a Spaniard, brought forth my country
    in my youth by Lord Soranzo's father, whom, whilst he
    lived I served faithfully; since whose death I have been to
    this man, as I was to him. What I have done was duty,
    and I repent nothing but that the loss of my life had not   120
    ransomed his.

97–100   lineation ed. (prose in Q)
 100   *thee* ed. (the Q)
 119   *this man* Soranzo

CARDINAL

    Say, fellow, know'st thou any yet unnamed

    Of counsel in this incest?

VASQUES

    Yes, an old woman, sometimes guardian to this murdered

    lady.   125

CARDINAL

    And what's become of her?

VASQUES

    Within this room she is, whose eyes after her confession I

    caused to be put out, but kept alive, to confirm what from Gio-

    vanni's own mouth you have heard. Now, my lord, what

    I have done you may judge of, and let your own wisdom be a judge   130

    in your own reason.

CARDINAL

    Peace! First, this woman, chief in these effects,

    My sentence is that forthwith she be ta'en

    Out of the city, for example's sake,

    There to be burnt to ashes.

DONADO   'Tis most just.   135

CARDINAL

    Be it your charge, Donado, see it done.

DONADO

    I shall.

VASQUES

    What for me? If death, 'tis welcome. I have been honest to the son

    as I was to the father.

CARDINAL

    Fellow, for thee: since what thou didst was done   140

    Not for thyself, being no Italian,

    We banish thee for ever, to depart

---

123 *Of counsel* Complicit

124 *sometimes* formerly

132 *this woman* It is unclear whether this means Putana or the dead Annabella, who is more obviously 'chief [i.e. principal] in these effects'. Either way, the Cardinal focuses the primary blame on a character who has been disempowered either by gender or rank: Annabella's body is given an admonitory cremation but Giovanni's is spared; or, alternatively, the servant Putana is made a scapegoat as the 'chief' criminal when she was really only an accomplice.

Within three days; in this we do dispense
With grounds of reason, not of thine offence.
VASQUES
    'Tis well: this conquest is mine, and I rejoice that a Spaniard out-   145
went an Italian in revenge.   *Exit*
CARDINAL
    Take up these slaughtered bodies, see them buried;
    And all the gold and jewels, or whatsoever,
    Confiscate by the canons of the Church,
    We seize upon to the Pope's proper use.   150
                    [RICHARDETTO *takes off his disguise*]
RICHARDETTO
    Your grace's pardon: thus long I lived disguised
    To see the effect of pride and lust at once
    Brought both to shameful ends.
CARDINAL
    What, Richardetto, whom we thought for dead?
DONADO
    Sir, was it you –
RICHARDETTO   Your friend.
CARDINAL   We shall have time   155
    To talk at large of all; but never yet
    Incest and murder have so strangely met.
    Of one so young, so rich in Nature's store,
    Who could not say, 'Tis pity she's a whore?
                            Exeunt [*with the bodies*]

143–4 *dispense . . . offence* The Cardinal grants Vasques a legal dispensation (in commuting the
    death penalty to banishment) in recognition of the nature of his motives ('reason'), but
    this does not diminish the gravity of the offence itself.
145–6 *I rejoice . . . revenge* Vasques takes it as a point of national pride that he has outdone an
    Italian in a field where Italians were considered pre-eminent. It is unclear whether the
    particular Italian he has in mind is Giovanni or Soranzo (who begins 'to turn Italian' at
    V.iv.28); if the latter, then the previously devoted servant is showing a new independ-
    ence of mind now that his obligations to the Soranzo family are done.
148 *all the . . . jewels* Florio, Giovanni, and Soranzo have all died without heirs to inherit their
    property.
150 *proper* personal
156 *at large* in full
158 *Nature's store* the gifts of abundant Nature. The image was often used in connection with
    beautiful women; compare William Barksted and Lewis Machin, *The Insatiate Countess*,
    IV.ii.182: 'Thou abstract drawn from Nature's . . . storehouse'
159 Q *FINIS* omitted ed.

PRINTER'S AFTERWORD

The general commendation deserved by the actors in their presentment of this tragedy may easily excuse such few faults as are escaped in the printing: a common charity may allow him the ability of spelling, whom a secure confidence assures that he cannot ignorantly err in the application of sense.

5

2 *presentment* presentation on stage
2–3 *faults . . . escaped* uncorrected misprints
3–5 *a common . . . sense* if you accept that a person understands the meaning of the words he uses, it is only fair to assume that he knows how to spell them

APPENDIX

List of Characters from the 1633 Quarto

THE SCENE

PARMA

THE ACTORS' NAMES

Bonaventura,	A Friar
A Cardinal,	Nuncio to the Pope
Soranzo,	A Nobleman
Florio,	A Citizen of *Parma*
Donado,	Another Citizen
Grimaldi,	A Roman Gentleman
Giovanni,	Son to *Florio*
Bergetto,	Nephew to *Donado*
Richardetto,	A supposed Physician
Vasques,	Servant to *Soranzo*
Poggio,	Servant to *Bergetto*
Banditti	

WOMEN

Annabella,	Daughter to *Florio*
Hippolita,	Wife to *Richardetto*
Philotis,	His Niece
Putana,	Tutoress to *Annabella*

This list is authorial: it shares its distinctive layout with similar lists in four other Ford Quartos (*The Broken Heart, Love's Sacrifice, Perkin Warbeck,* and *The Lady's Trial*) from various different printers and publishers. Ford tended to order his characters hierarchically, here with churchmen at the top and women at the bottom. Within this structure three factors determine the characters' precise positioning: social standing (so that Soranzo, an aristocrat, is above the gentlemen, who are in turn above the servants); age (so that Florio and Donado are above Giovanni); and moral worth (so that the Friar, though technically junior to the Cardinal, stands at the head). Richardetto's lowly place is especially intriguing.